On Target English
Sentence and Word Skills

Year 6

Hilary Frost
Sarah Lindsay
Heather Painter

Edinburgh Gate
Harlow Essex

Contents

Black Beauty

Nouns and pronouns

Sentence work

- To revise common and proper nouns and pronouns

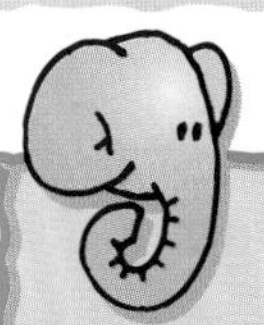

Remember

Nouns are sometimes called **naming** words.

Proper nouns start with a capital letter, and are the special name of a person, pet animal, place, day or month.

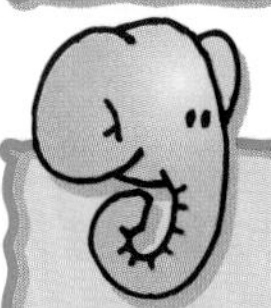

Remember

The prefix ***pro*** often means **in place of**.

There was a ploughboy, Dick, who sometimes came into our field. He picked blackberries from the hedge.

- A **common noun** is the name of something, like *field*, *hedge*.
- A **proper noun** is a special naming word, like Dick.
- A **pronoun** can be used **in place of a noun**, like *he*. (In this sentence *He* stands in place of *Dick*.)

Here are some other pronouns we often use:

I   you   him   it   she   he   they   we

1 Copy these sentences, and underline the common nouns in one colour and the proper nouns in another:

a Anna Sewell wrote a book called Black Beauty.

b Black Beauty was a horse.

c There was a ploughboy on the farm called Dick.

d Dick threw sticks and stones at the colts.

e The master told Dick he did not want him working on the farm.

f Old Daniel, who looked after the horses, was gentle and kind.

2 Copy the pronouns in each of these sentences:

a She wrote it many years ago.

b He said they thought it was good.

c We wish she had written another.

d You can borrow it.

e Can I have it back when you have finished?

Punctuation practice

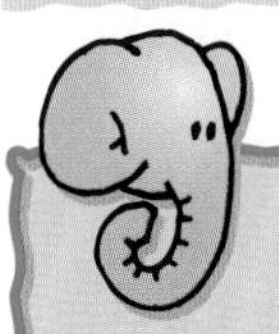

Sentence work

- To revise the key sentence punctuation

1 Each of these sentences is a statement, a question or an exclamation. Copy these statements and add the missing capital letters and punctuation marks.

a *we all liked old daniel*
b *ouch that hurt me*
c *we were not unkind to him*
d *why was dick so unkind to us*
e *i saw the master box his ears*

Remember

Statement sentences end with a **.**
questions with a **?**
and exclamations with a **!**

2 Copy this short paragraph, adding all the punctuation marks and captial letters that have been left out:

dick the ploughboy was unkind but not really a wicked person so black beauty was sorry when he lost his job but pleased that the horses wouldnt get hurt by the stones anymore daniel said he was pleased the master had fired dick

Adding *ing* and *ed*

Word work

- To learn spelling rules

Remember, to add ***ing*** or ***ed*** to a short word, look at the letter before the last letter.
If it is a short vowel sound, double the last letter before adding the suffix, like this:
hop hopping hopped
If the letter before the last letter is not a short vowel sound, just add the suffix, like this:
jump jumping *shout shouting*
a consonant **a double vowel**

Tip

If the last letters of a word are ***w***, ***x*** or ***y*** they are never doubled.

1 **a** Add *ing* to each of these words:
sit skip slip tap cut shut flap run shop
b Add *ed* to each of these words:
drop flip slip spot trap flap skip fret chop

2 **a** Add *ing* to each of these words:
wish slap dry wet spill fall kick trust catch
b Add *ed* to each of these words:
splash spot hoot start play harm look shop climb

Word work

- To recognise that words and expressions change over time

Old English / new English

As time passes, so does our language.
New words are needed (like **computer**, **e-mail**) and we no longer use some other words (like **ploughboy**).
Also, the way we pronounce some words gradually changes, and so does their spelling, e.g.
ceme (300 years ago) is now spelt *came*
sarten (300 years ago) is now spelt *certain*

Helpful words

will should
come are
has gave
spoke shall
says

1 Write the modern version of each of these verbs.
The first is done to help you.

a cometh come
b spake
c gavest
d art
e shalt
f hath
g saith
h wilt
i shouldst

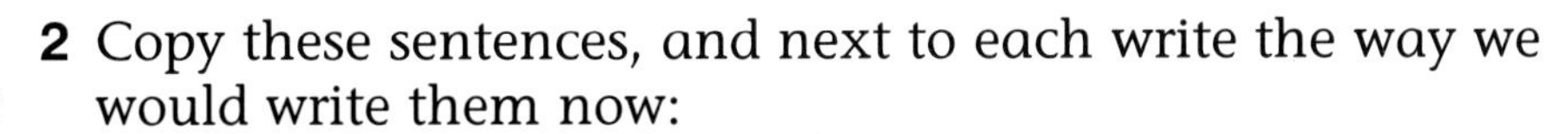

2 Copy these sentences, and next to each write the way we would write them now:

a Cometh ye hither.

b Wilt thou cometh nigh that I might glance upon thee?

c Thou shalt abide with my kin in this dwelling.

d I wast in the midst of mine adversaries!

Helpful words

ye = you
thee = you
thou = you
adversaries = enemies
abide = live
in the midst = among
kin = family
mine = my
nigh = near

a + double letter patterns

Handwriting

acc ann all ass arr acc ann all ass arr

1 a Practise the letter patterns three times.

b Neatly copy these words twice each:

accurate accuse annoy announce

allow allergy assistant assembly

arrest arrive

2 a Neatly copy the silly sentence:

I was embarrassed and annoyed when the assistant arrived late.

b Make your own sentence that must include all of these words:

accountant arrange arrest allow

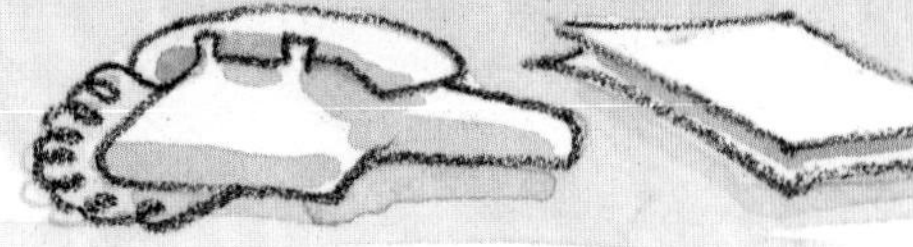

Unit 2

Famous Victorians

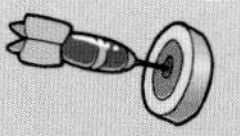

Sentence work

- To revise collective and abstract nouns

Collective and abstract nouns

Tunnel and *bridge* are **common nouns** and *Brunel* and *London* are **proper nouns**.
Here are two other sorts of nouns:
Team and *crowd* are **collective nouns**. They are names for collections of people or things.
Opposition and *kindness* are **abstract nouns**.
They are names of things, such as ideas and feelings, that you can't see, touch or smell.

Helpful words

flock gang
crowd herd

1 Which collective noun would you use instead of **lot** in these phrases?

a a lot of people

b a lot of sheep

c a lot of cattle

d a lot of workmen

2 a Copy out the abstract nouns from each of these sets of words:

- excitement grass magic bread belief thought
- curiosity sugar flame fact opinion agreement
- happiness sorrow joy animal anger

b Abstract nouns can be made by adding suffixes such as *ness*, *ment* and *ion*. Write the abstract nouns which can be formed from these words. The first is done for you.

dark <u>darkness</u> improve object

like pay enjoy act involve

c Write sentences using these abstract nouns:

excitement curiosity attitude

Punctuation practice

1 Each of these sentences is a statement or a question. Add the missing capital letters and punctuation marks.

a when was brunel born

b he was born in 1806

c why was the invention of steam locomotives important in the story of brunel

d steam locomotives needed railways bridges tunnels and stations which brunel built

e did he build anything else

f yes he designed and constructed some large famous ships such as the great britain and the great eastern

2 Copy this short paragraph, adding all the punctuation marks and capital letters that have been left out:

after hed finished work on the tunnel under the river thames isambard kingdom brunel entered a competition to build a bridge across the river avon near bristol his winning entry which is now known as the clifton suspension bridge was a great feat and remains to this day a major landmark in bristol

Sentence work

- To revise the key sentence punctuation

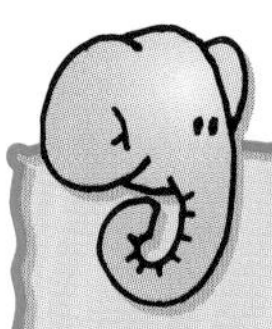

Remember

In a list, commas should be used, except before *and* at the end of the list.

Remember

We put a comma in long sentences where we want the reader to make a short pause.

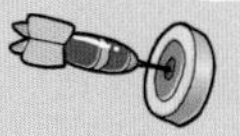

Word work

- To introduce the concept of unstressed vowels

Tip

We sometimes miss out unstressed vowels when we are spelling words.

Word work

- To consider the origins of some nouns

Unstressed vowels

Say these words aloud:

difference chocolate company

When these words are said aloud, the letters underlined are hard to hear. They are called **unstressed** vowels.

1 Copy these words. Circle the unstressed vowels.

a vegetables **b** interest
c temperature **d** business
e factory **f** dictionary
g entrance **h** valuable

2 Use a dictionary to help you spot the unstressed vowels that have been left out of these words. Write the correct spelling:

a silntly **b** diffrent
c assistnce **d** necessry
e secretry **f** Febrary
g nursry **h** prisner

Names

Some **common** and **proper** nouns have come from other nouns:

- some are named after objects in our universe: Monday (*moon*day)
- some are named after Roman emperors: July (*Jul*ius Caesar)
- some are named after famous people: Ford motor cars (Henry *Ford*)
- many place names were first made by the Anglo-Saxons (*ham* = settlement in Old English)

1 Draw a small picture of the thing that each of these people gave their name to:

a Duke of Wellington **b** Laszlo Biro
c Adolphe Sax **d** The 4th Earl of Sandwich

2 a Use dictionaries and encyclopedias to find the origins of these words:

guillotine cardigan Pennsylvania Braille

Helpful words

Thursday February
April Saturday
August October

b Name the day or month that gets its name from:

Emperor Augustus

Saturn, the Roman god and planet

the Latin word *aprilis* (meaning when buds open)

the Roman number eight, *octo*

Thor, the god of thunder

Februa, the Roman festival

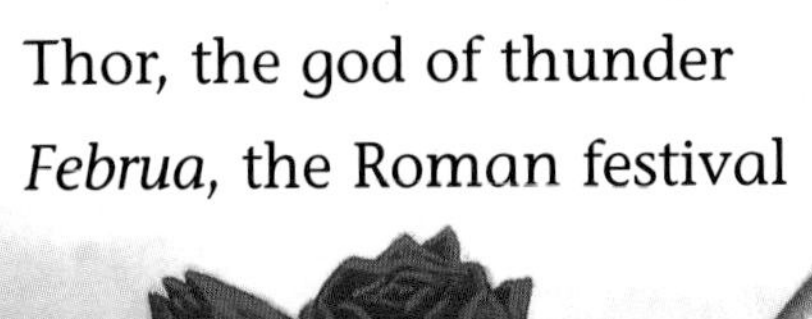

c Match the Old English words in the box with these place names.

feld = open land	*ford* = river crossing	*burh* = fort
tun = farm or village	*ingas* = followers of	

Macclesfield Oxford Moreton Reading Canterbury

ance, ence and *ince* patterns

Handwriting

ance ence ince ance ence ince ance ence ince

1 a Practise the letter patterns three times.

b Neatly copy these words twice each:

distance fragrance silence
difference since wince

2 Check in a dictionary whether to add *ance* or *ence* to each of these letters to make a word. Then neatly copy them twice each.

a *consequ* **b** *import*
c *abs* **d** *extravag*

The Sea

Sentence work

- To revise adjectives and adjective phrases

Helpful words

large colourful
chubby cheerful
noisy big
red blue
small green
dangerous

Adjectives

Remember, **adjectives** describe nouns:

shaggy jaws — **adjective** *noun*
sandy shores — **adjective** *noun*

Sometimes we need an **adjective phrase** to describe a noun:

The dog, his long hair soaking wet, shook himself all over my gran!

his long hair soaking wet is an **adjective phrase**.

1 Look at the picture. Write two adjectives to describe each of these nouns. The first is done for you.

a tall, dangerous cliffs
b ______ beachball
c ______ kite
d ______ waves
e ______ baby

2 a Copy these sentences and neatly underline the adjective phrase in each one. Put a circle around the noun that is being described.

The beach, soft and sandy, was just right for making castles.

One of the waves, huge, foaming and powerful, knocked Dad off his feet.

Gran, always kind and forgiving, laughed and gave the dog a pat.

The sun, too hot for comfort, shone all day.

b Use these adjective phrases in sentences of your own:

dark, damp and in danger of collapse

big and brightly coloured

Contractions

Remember, a **contraction** is when we leave out some letters and put an **apostrophe** (') in their place.

The sea is a hungry dog

The sea's a hungry dog

So, **sea's** is a contraction for **sea is.**

The **apostrophe** shows where **i** has been left out as the two words have been put together.

1 Write the contraction for each of these:

a she is **b** do not

c should not **d** I have

e there is **f** has not

g we are **h** it is

i cannot **j** will not

2 Copy these sentences, putting a contraction for the words underlined:

a The dog would not go away to shake himself!

b "I will take him away, Gran," I said.

c "Do not worry," Gran laughed, "I am soaked already."

d "You are so wet you might as well go for a swim," I suggested.

e "Come on, let us have a dip in the sea," she said.

Sentence work

- To revise apostrophes for contractions

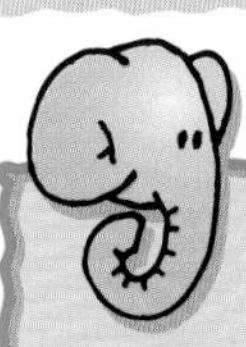

Remember

Contract means to *get smaller.*

Tip

The apostrophe goes exactly where the missing letters would have been.

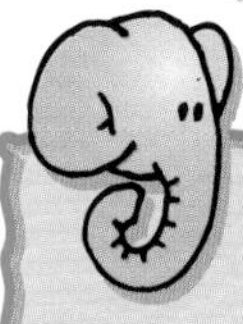

Remember

Sometimes some of the letters in the word change when it contracts.

Helpful words

hasn't wouldn't
shouldn't it's
I've we're
won't she's
don't I'm
there's can't
let's you're

Word work

- To practise using a dictionary to check spellings

Dictionary practice

1 Use your dictionary to correct these words, all of which are spelt incorrectly:

a jorney	**b** intresting
c exsiting	**d** matirial
e center	**f** requied
g succesful	**h** engins
i capeable	**j** incluеding
k carriges	**l** invension

2 Write your own definition of each of these words, and then write the dictionary definition:

a tide **b** cliff **c** boulder

Word work

- To explore how new words are added to our language

New words for new things

New words are needed to name new inventions, new fashions and new games.

1 Name ten things in the picture that people born 200 years ago would not have known.

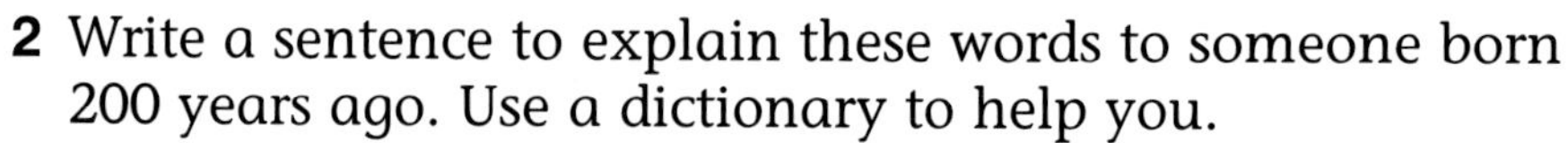

2 Write a sentence to explain these words to someone born 200 years ago. Use a dictionary to help you.

a satellite	**b** computer
c jeans	**d** sneakers
e vacuum cleaner	**f** television

Setting out

1 Find a poem about the sea. Use the verse below if you wish. As well as writing it neatly, think carefully about how you will place it on the page. Leave sufficient space around it so that you can illustrate or decorate it later.

2 Using a ruler, draw a border around your poem. Measure the border to make it neat and regular. Finally, add some illustration or decoration.

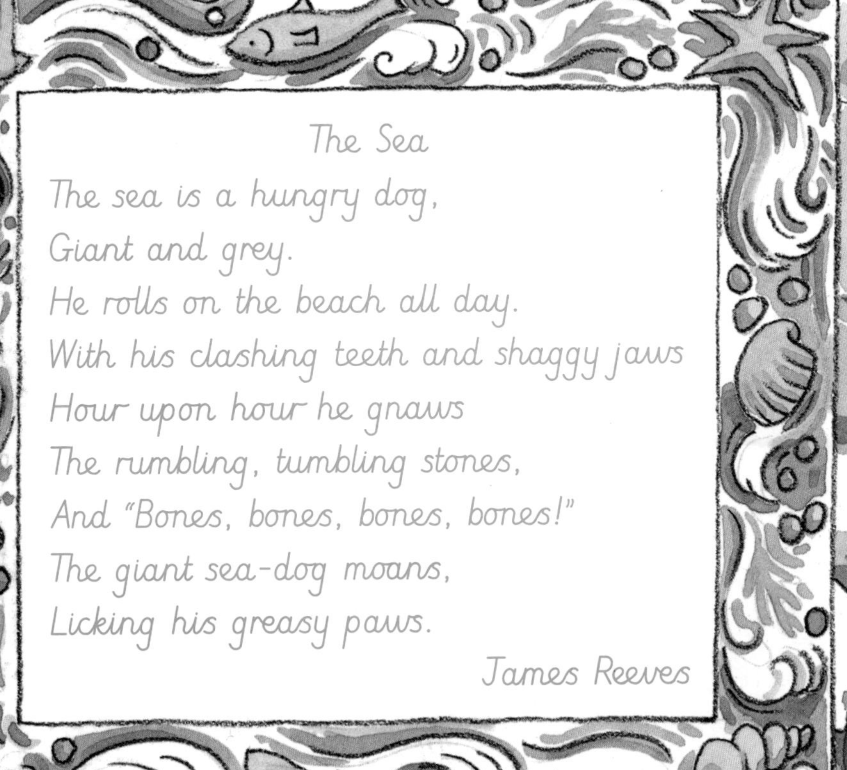

Tom's Midnight Garden

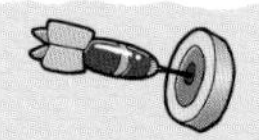

Sentence work

- To revise verbs and adverbs

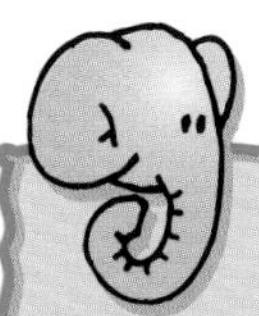

Remember

Verbs are often called **doing** words.

Being and having verbs are sometimes called **helper** or **auxiliary** verbs.

Adverbs *add* to our information about *verbs*.

They tell us **how**, **when** or **where** the action of a verb takes place.

Helpful words

looking weeding
shoving pushing
glaring staring
digging angrily
irritably frustratedly
neatly carefully

Verbs and adverbs

The gardener had emptied his barrow-load of weeds and was sitting on the handle of his barrow.

The words underlined are **verbs**. Most verbs are used for actions, but some verbs are about being or having, such as *was* and *had*. These can sometimes *help* the action verb.

Adverbs can tell us how actions happen. They describe verbs.

The gardener sat wearily.

1 Write a sentence with a verb and an adverb about each of these pictures. Neatly underline the verbs in red and the adverbs in blue.

a

b

c

2 a Many adverbs, describing **how** actions are done, end with *ly*. Write three *ly* adverbs that could be used with each of these verbs. The first one is done for you.

run quickly slowly swiftly

shout think eat walk

b Write a sentence for each of the above verbs. Use at least one of your adverbs with each verb.

Punctuating speech

Sentence work

- To practise punctuating dialogue sentences

Remember, speech marks go around the words in a sentence that were actually spoken:

"I'm going through," Tom gasped.

1 Copy these sentences, adding the missing speech marks:

a I enjoyed reading the book about Tom, said Kirsty.

b So did I, replied Ali.

c The best bit was when he tried to get through the gate, Kirsty added.

d I've had funny dreams like that, said Ali.

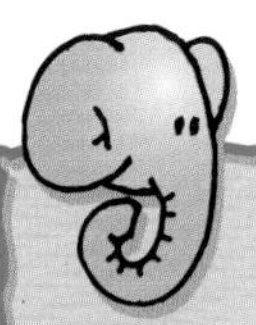

Remember

A comma comes at the end of the words spoken, but *before* the second speech marks.

2 In these sentences the commas, other punctuation marks and capital letters have all been left out. Copy them as they should be written.

a how do you think tom felt when the door was locked asked kirsty

b pretty fed up i should say answered ali

c yes i would have been really cross said his friend

d just imagine said ali what fun we could have if we could walk through doors

e wouldnt it be great to be invisible said Kirsty excitedly

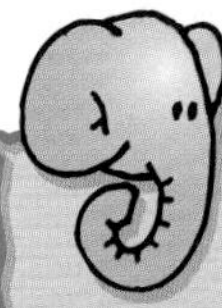

Remember

In spoken questions we use a question mark instead of a comma before the speech marks.

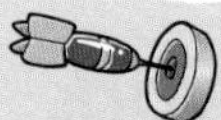

Word work

- To revise and extend knowledge of prefixes

Prefixes

Tom's fingers were quite <u>un</u>hurt.

Remember, prefixes are added to the beginnings of words. They change the meaning of, or give more information about, the root word.

Remember

A prefix added to a root word does not change the spelling of the main word.

1 Copy these words and underline the prefixes:

a *aeroplane* **b** *aqualung*
c *bicycle* **d** *hydrofoil*
e *injustice* **f** *microscope*
g *impossible* **h** *photograph*
i *submarine* **j** *telephone*
k *tricycle* **l** *export*

2 a Select prefixes from those you underlined to add to each of these roots:

___*decisive* ___*modest* ___*vision*

___*angle* ___*change* ___*electric*

___*way* ___*merge* ___*ability*

b What do each of these prefixes mean? The first is done for you.

bi = *two* sub

tri oct

aqua micro

Word work

- To consider the differences between synonyms

Choosing between synonyms

Remember, synonyms are words or phrases that have the same or a similar meaning.

pretty *attractive* *beautiful* *lovely* *dainty* *pleasing*

Each of these words has a slightly different meaning, so we need to think carefully about which word to use when we are writing.

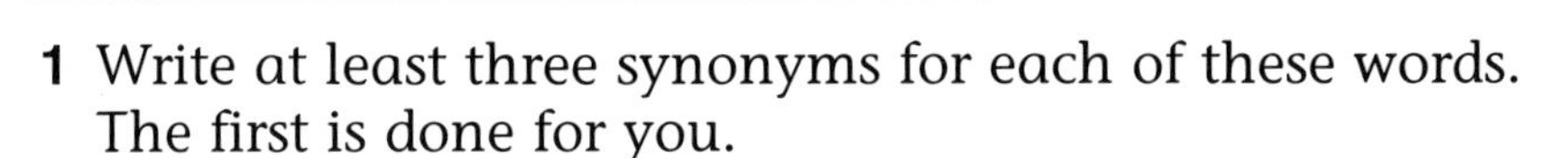

1 Write at least three synonyms for each of these words. The first is done for you.

a look: *see watch gaze stare observe*

b delicious

c climb

d take

e move

f tiny

2 Find each of these pairs of words in a dictionary. Write sentences to show that you know the differences between them.

a *special unique* **b** *plenty copious*

c *ask summon* **d** *ignore neglect*

Handwriting

aero, *micro* and *hydro* prefixes

aero micro hydro aero micro hydro

1 **a** Write these prefixes very neatly three times.

b Neatly copy these words twice each:

aerobics aerofoil microchip
microdot hydroelectric hydrogen

2 Use a dictionary to find three other words that begin with each of the prefixes. Copy them neatly into your book.

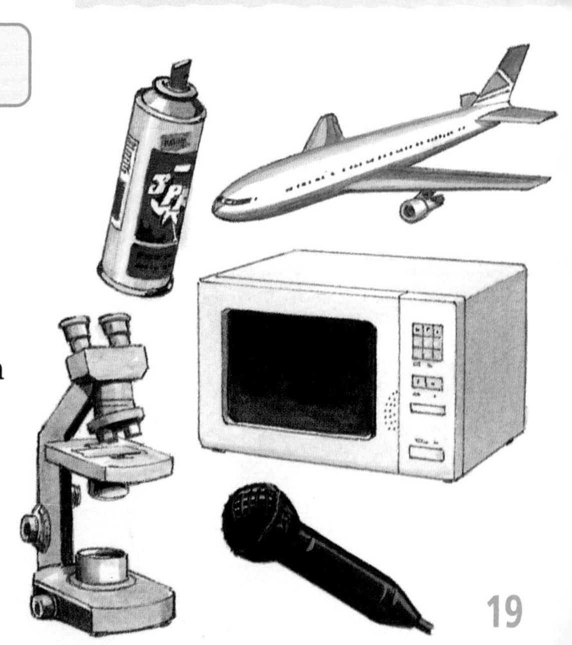

Unit 5

Two fables

Sentence work

- To practise identifying and selecting prepositions

Prepositions

Prepositions tell us the **position** of something, e.g.

Nothing at all appeared <u>on</u> its branches.

Remember

Antonyms are opposites.

1 a Copy the prepositions in these two boxes. Match the antonyms.

outside from up over on before below

under off down above inside to after

b Write this sentence so that it has three different meanings, just by using different prepositions:

The fig tree grew ______ the hill.

up the ladder
in the basket
off the tree
on the ground
from the village

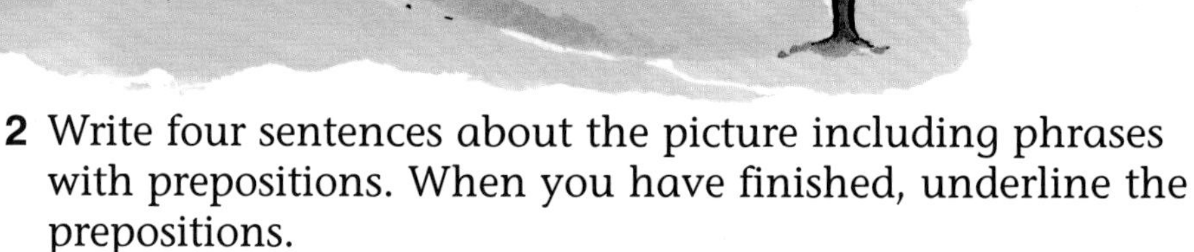

2 Write four sentences about the picture including phrases with prepositions. When you have finished, underline the prepositions.

Using commas in sentences

Sentence work

- To practise using commas in longer sentences

We put a comma where we want our readers to take a short pause in long, complicated sentences and in sentences using direct speech, e.g.

So without thinking too much about it, the flea moved house, leaping from the dog's coat to the sheep's fleece.

1 Copy these sentences, putting commas where you think the reader should make a short pause:

a A flea who lived in the smooth hair of a dog one day noticed the pleasant smell of wool.

b "That fleece is exactly what I need" said the flea.

c He tried and tried patiently separating one strand from another laboriously making a way through.

2 Remember, we also use commas after **Yes** and **No** at the beginning of a sentence. Copy these sentences, putting commas wherever they are needed:

a "Yes I think I'll move home" thought the flea.

b "Yes that fleece looks just right" he said.

c No the flea was not happy in his new home.

d No the flea could not get back to the dog.

Remember

In direct speech, the comma is put before the second speech marks.

Word work

- To be more aware of silent letters

Silent letters

> The fig tree had no delicious fruit.
>
> Some letters don't make a sound when read, like ***i*** in *delicious* and *fruit*.

1 These words look wrong. All the **silent** letters have been left out. Copy out the words, adding the missing letters where they are needed.

a lam bom dum crum thum clim det dout lim

b nit nob nelt nack nock nife neel nown nuckle

c rapper riggle rinkle rite reck rist sord anser

d weel wether wich wisker wisper wite onest ryme

e hym autum colum condem

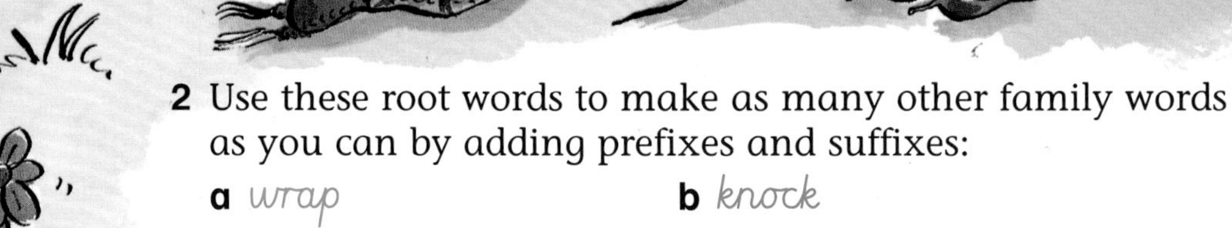

2 Use these root words to make as many other family words as you can by adding prefixes and suffixes:

a wrap
b knock
c know
d honest
e condemn
f climb

Building compound words

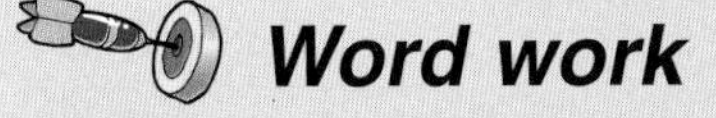

Word work

- To revise how compound words are built from shorter words

Everyone passed by without looking at it.

Compound words are words that are made from two shorter words joined together.

every + one = everyone   with + out = without

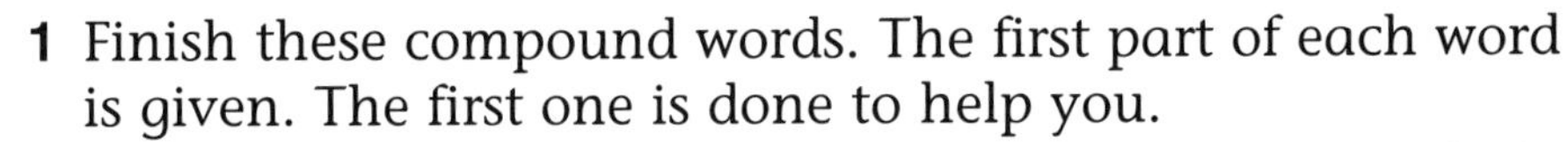

1 Finish these compound words. The first part of each word is given. The first one is done to help you.

a some something

b foot **c** farm

d play **e** spot

f home **g** table

h man **i** earth

Helpful words

earthworm farmhouse
tablecloth mankind
homework spotlight
playtime football

2 Make at least ten compound words, taking a word from each box.

some	every	goal	motor	match	any

way	where	keeper	one	box	thing

kn, *wr* and *mb* patterns

Handwriting

kn wr mb kn wr mb kn wr mb kn wr mb

1 **a** Practise the letter patterns three times.

b Neatly copy these words twice each:

knotted knitting knife

wriggly wrinkly wrapper

lamb crumb climb

2 Make an amusing sentence using as many of the nine words as you can from question 1.

Britain's Sharks Face Extinction

Sentence work

- To revise active and passive sentences

Active and passive sentences

Sentences are **active** when the person or thing the sentence is about *does* the action, e.g.

The fisherman caught a shark.

Sentences are **passive** when the person or thing the sentence is about has the action *done to it*, e.g.

A shark was caught by the fisherman.

Tip

The person or thing the sentence is about is called the **subject** of the sentence.

Tip

Notice that the active verbs in **passive sentences** need **helper verbs**.

1 Rewrite these sentences with the verb changed from active to passive, so that the person or thing the sentence is about has the action done to it. Underline the main verb and helper verb.

a Some people eat the shark's dorsal fin.

The shark's dorsal fin is eaten by some people.

b Fishermen slaughter the sharks.

c The fishermen sell the fins.

d Seaquest monitors the numbers of sharks being killed.

2 Now write these sentences with the verbs changed from passive to active:

a The expert was alarmed by the decline in basking shark numbers.

b Too many sharks were killed by the fishermen.

c A fisherman was bitten by a shark.

d Some restaurant owners are concerned by the situation.

Clauses

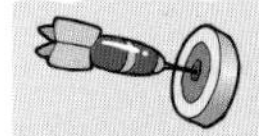

Sentence work

- To revise clauses

> Remember, a **clause** is a group of words with a **verb**. The clause can be used as a sentence or as part of a sentence.
>
> *Basking sharks visit Britain each summer.*
>
> This is a single-clause sentence with one verb.
>
> *Basking sharks visit Britain each summer as they swim between Iceland and Portugal.*
>
> This is a two-clause sentence with two verbs.

1 Copy these sentences. Underline the two clauses in each one. Circle the verb in each clause. The first one is done for you.

a *Sharks are facing extinction because too many are killed each year.*

Sharks (are facing) extinction / because too many (are killed) each year.

b *Basking sharks can weigh up to five tons but can jump two metres above the sea.*

c *The sharks are killed only for their fins, so the rest of the creature is dumped back into the sea.*

2 Add a second clause to each of these main clauses. Begin each with the conjunction that is underlined.

a *I never eat shark fin soup because*

b *We saw some basking sharks while*

c *Some fishermen have stopped catching sharks until*

d *It is difficult to be sure how many basking sharks there are so*

Tip

The clause that makes sense by itself is called the **main clause**.

Word work

- To practise recognising the main parts of a word to help spelling

Prefixes, roots and suffixes

There are three parts to many words.

endangered

Prefix = ***en*** Root = **danger** Suffix = ***ed***

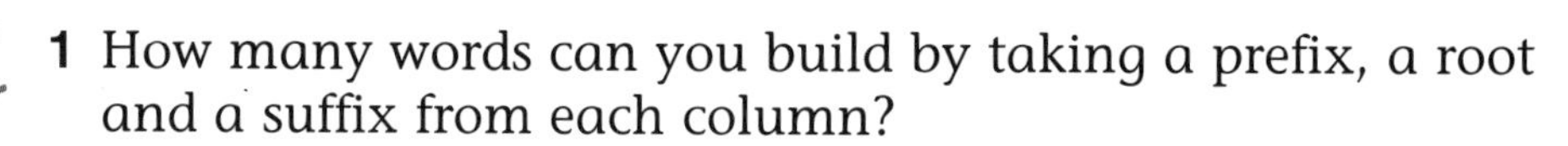

1 How many words can you build by taking a prefix, a root and a suffix from each column?

Prefixes	Roots	Suffixes
un	agree	ic
dis	concern	able
in	port	ing
im	press	ant
ex	graph	ible
photo	cred	ed

2 Use a dictionary to find two words that begin with each of these prefixes:

a aero **b** aqua **c** bi
d con **e** duo **f** hydro
g micro **h** oct **i** sub
j tele **k** trans **l** tri

Using synonyms

We need to choose from possible synonyms carefully, e.g.
big large **great huge enormous massive tremendous**
Fishermen slaughter the basking shark for its large dorsal fin.

1 Write as many synonyms as you can think of for each of the words underlined, and then underline the one you would choose to write in each case:
  a For centuries the basking shark has made a summer pilgrimage to Britain.
  b The creatures can be seen jumping two metres above the sea.
  c This splendid sight is becoming more rare.
  d Basking sharks are very vulnerable to hunting.
  e If you start killing them the numbers get fewer.

2 a Use a thesaurus to find synonyms for each of these words, and then write the words in order from the *most* to the *least*:
  pretty   rare   rich   fast
  b Write a sentence for the *least* in each of your sets of words.

Word work

- To revise why selecting appropriate synonyms is important

Remember

Synonyms are words or phrases that have similar meanings.

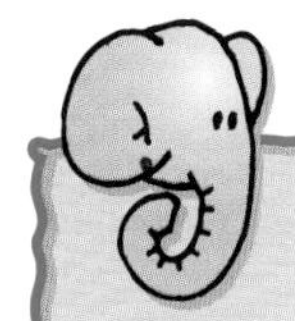

Remember

A synonym can be more than one word.

able, ible, ent and *ant* suffixes

able ible ent ant able ible ent ant able ible ent ant

1 a Practise the letter patterns three times.
  b Neatly copy these words twice each:
  lovable valuable horrible terrible
  silent obedient ignorant elegant

2 a Neatly copy this silly jingle:
  The lovable puppy had a horrible master.
  However quickly he walked, he made him go faster.
  b Make your own funny rhyme that uses at least two words ending in *able*, *ible*, *ent* or *ant*.

Handwriting

Unit 7

The Children of the New Forest

Sentence work

- To revise the use of conjunctions

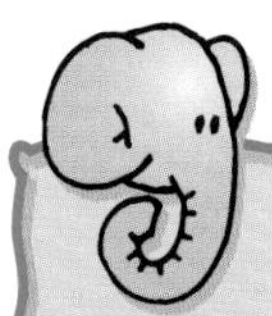

Remember

Conjunctions such as *and*, *but*, *because*, *although* are sometimes called **joining words**. They are useful when we join short sentences.

Helpful words

and but
so because
although though
after for
until yet
then as
or when
while so

Conjunctions

> *The troopers sat down to the table, and very soon the whole contents of the kettle had disappeared.*

These two short sentences have been joined by a **conjunction**, *and*.

1 Join each of these sentences with conjunctions to make single sentences:

a The children have been hidden. Their father's enemies are nearby.

b The troopers are approaching the cottage. Jacob sends the children upstairs.

c They didn't look at the children. They didn't want to catch smallpox!

d Jacob was happy to let the troopers eat the food. It kept them happy.

e After the troopers had gone, Jacob cooked more food. They were all very hungry before it was ready.

2 Take each of these short sentences, choose a conjunction, and add another clause to make it longer and more interesting:

a The four children could hear the troopers searching ...

b They kept very still and quiet ...

c Humphrey could hear the troopers eating their dinner ...

d Jacob said it was a small price to pay ...

e The children all agreed ...

Practising dialogue

When writing dialogue, it is important to remember to begin a new line when a different person starts to speak.

"Come in," said Jacob.
"Who are you, my friend?" said the leader of the troop, entering the door.
"A poor forester, sir," replied Jacob, "under great trouble."

1 Copy each of these sentences, adding the missing speech marks, commas and apostrophes:

a All the children are in bed with smallpox said Jacob.

b Please dont disturb them added Jacob as they are very ill.

c We must search every cottage said the troop leader barging past Jacob

d Theres no one here said one of the troopers Shall we be off?

e Wait a while said the captain for Im hungry and I can smell something rather tasty.

2 Rewrite this short paragraph, starting a new line when a different person begins to speak. Add the missing speech marks and commas.

That food smells good said the captain I should like a spoonful or two. You are welcome said Jacob I will cook some more for myself. My, that was good said the youngest trooper. Can I have some more? You may said Jacob and very welcome I'm sure.

Sentence work

- To revise dialogue punctuation

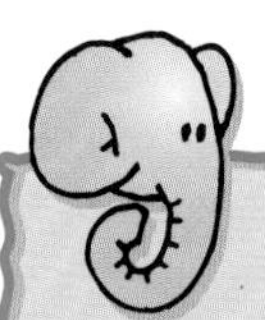

Remember

Dialogue is spoken words and sentences.

Tip

Look out for missing apostrophes!

Tip

Notice how the speech marks are outside the full stops and commas.

Word work

- To practise some tricky spellings

Double consonants

One of the trickiest things about spelling is remembering when to use double letters!

Very soon the whole dinner in the kettle had disappeared, and just when they had a big appetite!

1 Hidden in this wordsearch are the answers to these riddles. All the answers have double letters.

a	s	s	e	m	b	l	y	a	s
p	a	t	t	a	c	k	a	x	c
p	d	t	o	p	s	i	p	c	b
l	d	o	p	p	o	n	e	n	t
a	l	r	p	e	x	n	a	d	m
u	e	v	o	a	s	s	i	s	t
s	d	c	n	r	p	z	s	a	t
e	a	n	n	u	a	l	s	d	a
q	u	a	r	r	e	l	t	d	c
d	i	f	f	e	r	e	n	t	k

a Another word for clapping.
b Antonym of defend.
c You need this to ride a horse.
d Antonym for same.
e Take off ap and you have a fruit.
f Synonym for help.
g To argue.
h When all the school meets together.
i Happens once a year.
j Someone you are competing against.

2 Write five more words which have double letters.

Our changing language

The words we use, and the way we use them, are always changing. The author has written this dialogue as these people might have spoken over 300 years ago.

"Who are you, my friend?" said the leader of the troop.
"A poor forester, sir," replied Jacob, "under great trouble."
"What trouble, my man?"

1 Write the dialogue in the box, but as it would be spoken today.

2 What words or phrases do we now use instead of these?

a yonder
b ye
c tarry awhile
d thou art bidden
e it was bestowed upon me
f What saith thou?

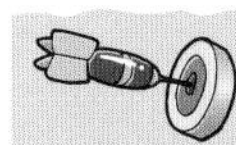

Word work

- To raise awareness of how language changes over time

Remember

Dialogue is conversation that is written.

a + double letter patterns

app abb add aff agg att

1 **a** Practise the letter patterns three times.
b Neatly copy these words twice each:
apple dabble saddle raffle gaggle battle

2 **a** Neatly list at least one word (more if you can!) that rhymes with each of the six words you have copied in question 1.
b Make an amusing sentence using as many double letter words as you can.

Handwriting

Prince Cinders

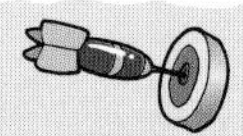

Sentence work

- To make sure nouns and verbs match, both being plural or singular

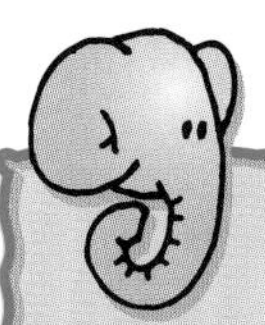

Remember

Is and **are** are in the **present tense**; **was** and **were** are **past tense** verbs.

Tip

We use **were** or **are** next to the word *you* whether it is referring to one or more than one person.

Matching nouns and verbs

Prince Cinders was not much of a prince.

We usually use **was** or **is** if we are writing about *one* person or thing.

He had three brothers who were always teasing him about his looks

We use **were** or **are** if we are writing about *more than one* person or thing.

1 Copy these sentences, choosing the correct verb:

a Prince Cinders (was/were) small.

b He (was/were) also scruffy and skinny.

c His brothers (was/were) always being unkind.

d There (was/were) various reasons for their unkindness.

e It made Prince Cinders wish he (was/were) big and hairy like his brothers.

f "Why (is/are) you unhappy?" asked the fairy.

g "My brothers (is/are) so cruel to me," answered the young prince.

h "You (is/are) a fine prince," said the fairy.

i "You (is/are) silly to worry about them," she added.

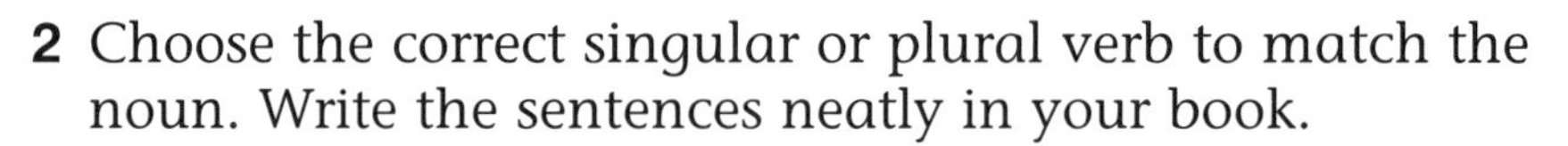

2 Choose the correct singular or plural verb to match the noun. Write the sentences neatly in your book.

a The brothers (make/makes) Cinders stay at home.

b Prince Cinders (wash/washes) the dirty socks.

c He (wish/wishes) he could go to the disco.

d The fairy (turn/turns) Prince Cinders into a monkey!

e The spell (wear/wears) off at midnight.

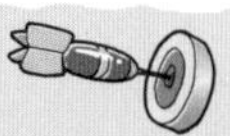

Sentence work

- To introduce main and subordinate clauses

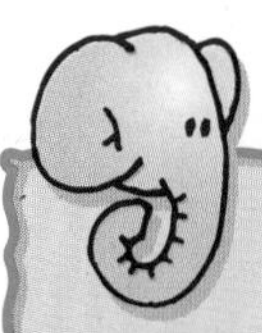

Tip

Subordinate means *less important*.

Remember

The main clause must make sense by itself.

Types of clauses

He had three big hairy brothers / who were always teasing him about his looks.

He had three big hairy brothers is a **main clause** because it makes sense by itself.

who were always teasing him about his looks is a **subordinate clause** because it tells us more about the main clause and doesn't make sense by itself.

Subordinate clauses are often joined to main clauses by conjunctions or pronouns, such as:

because although when so until before but (*conjunctions*)

who whose which that (*pronouns*)

1 Write the main clause in each of these sentences:

a *Prince Cinders had three big brothers who were always saying unkind things.*

b *The car was too small to drive but he made the best of it.*

c *Prince Cinders did not know he was a big hairy monkey because that was the kind of spell it was.*

2 Add a subordinate clause to make these sentences more interesting:

a *The fairy performed her spell (so) ...*

b *Prince Cinders thought he looked big and handsome (but) ...*

c *The prince managed to get out by midnight (although) ...*

Adding suffixes to short words

Remember, when adding a suffix to a short word, like **jog** or **bat**, if the letter *before the last* is a short vowel, the last letter is doubled.

jog	jogging
short vowel	double last letter + suffix
bat	batted

1 Add ing and er to these words. Decide whether you need to double the last letter before adding ing or er.

a scan scanning scanner
b shop
c drip
d hop
e hit
f fit
g sell
h chop
i cut
j bat
k tap
l let
m peck
n wrap
o chat
p begin

2 Write these words in the past tense by adding ed:

a drop
b nod
c slip
d wrap
e strap
f float
g slim
h row
i submit
j cancel
k crack
l dump

Word work

- To practise adding suffixes to words ending with a short vowel and single consonant

Tip

The rule also works for longer words, where the last syllable is stressed, as in trans**mit**/**transmitter**.

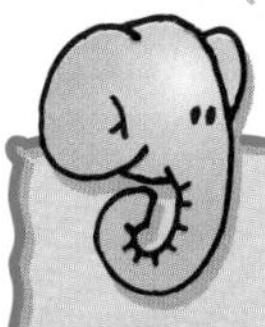

Remember

Syllables are sections of a word. Each syllable in a word has a vowel sound.

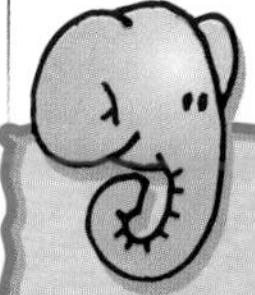

Remember

We never double ***w***, ***x*** or ***y***, not even for this rule!

Word work

- To introduce proverbs

Proverbs

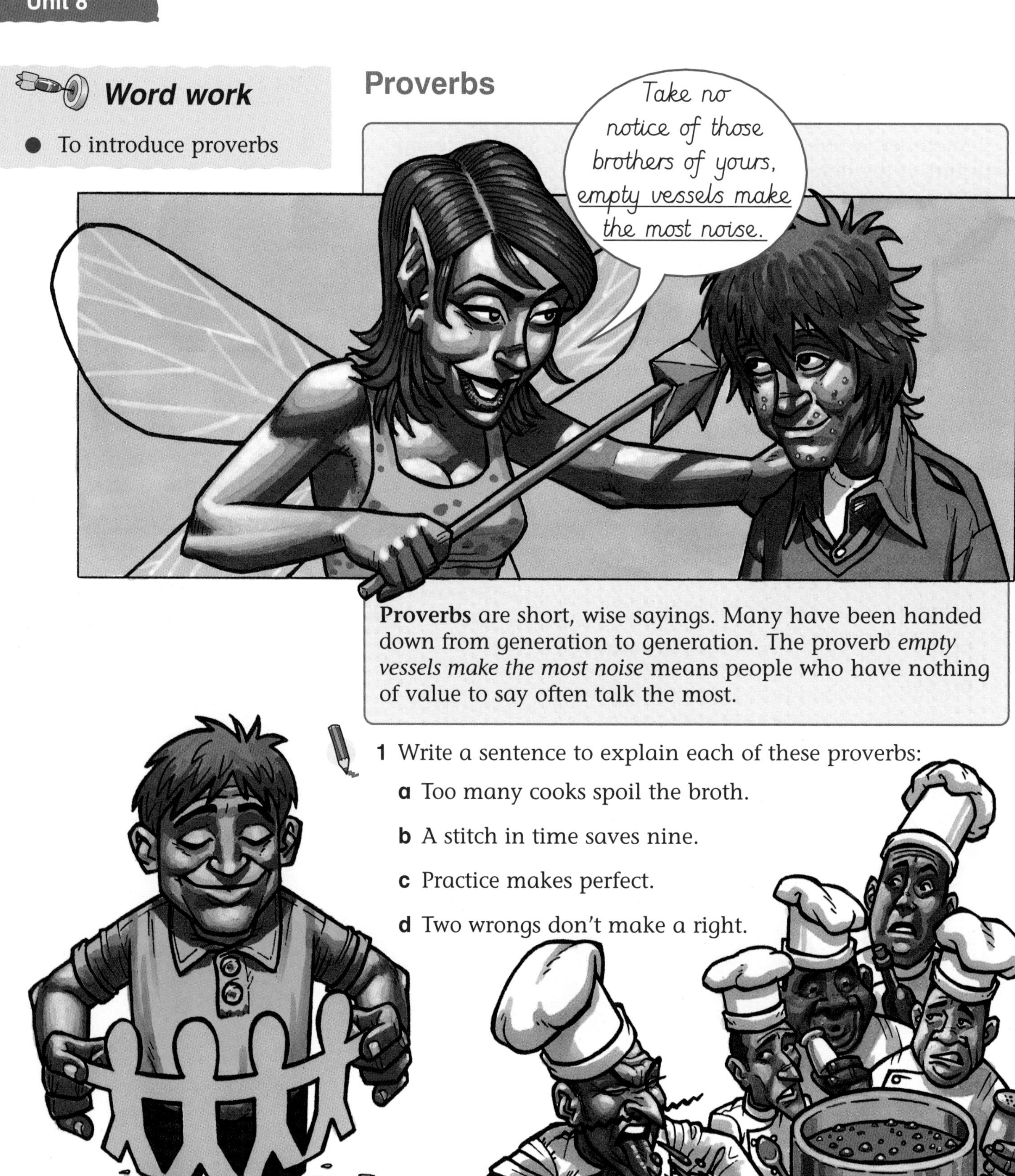

Proverbs are short, wise sayings. Many have been handed down from generation to generation. The proverb *empty vessels make the most noise* means people who have nothing of value to say often talk the most.

1 Write a sentence to explain each of these proverbs:

a Too many cooks spoil the broth.

b A stitch in time saves nine.

c Practice makes perfect.

d Two wrongs don't make a right.

2 a Write an ending for each of these proverbs:

When the cat's away …

More haste …

Let sleeping dogs …

Don't count your chickens …

b Write a short story that includes and explains one of the proverbs you have completed.

Helpful words

lie
the mice will play
before they're hatched
less speed

Practising layout

Handwriting

Neat handwriting is important if we want our reader to believe that what we have written is good and worth reading.

Layout is also important.

This means:

- using the space on the page thoughtfully
- not crowding our work
- using a ruler every time we need to draw a straight line

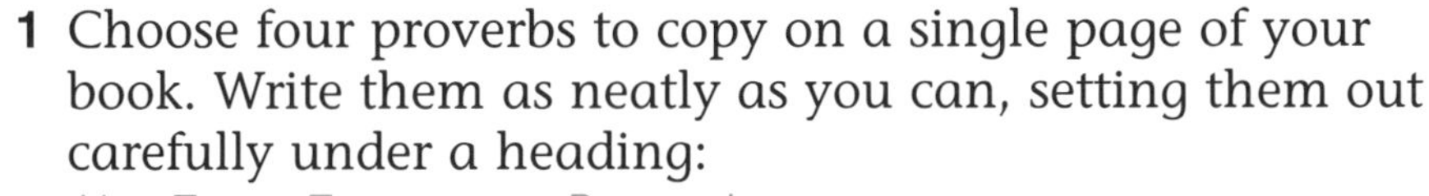

1 Choose four proverbs to copy on a single page of your book. Write them as neatly as you can, setting them out carefully under a heading:
My Four Favourite Proverbs.

2 Illustrate or decorate the page so that others would be attracted to it and want to look at it.

The Phantom Tollbooth

Sentence work

- To avoid using double negatives in sentences

Tip

Here are some common negatives:

no not _n't_ never nothing nowhere nobody

Double negatives

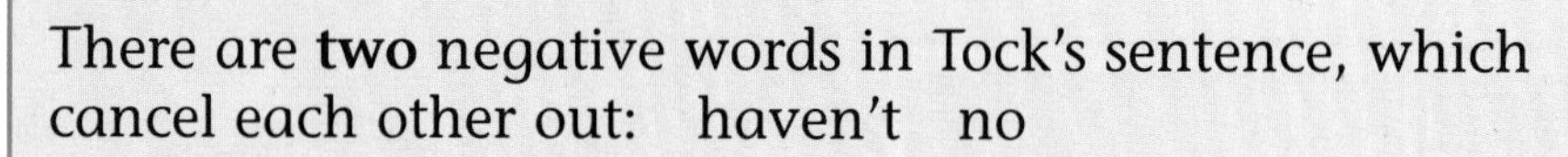

There are **two** negative words in Tock's sentence, which cancel each other out: haven't no

A sentence with two negative words becomes positive.

Think about it. If Tock hasn't **no** idea, he must have **some** idea!

1 Correct each of these negative sentences, so that they mean what the writer really intended.

a *I haven't no idea what he's talking about.*
I have no idea what he's talking about.

b *Tock didn't like no trouble.*

c *Milo didn't buy no letters from the man.*

d *He hadn't got no numbers, only letters.*

e *The bee hadn't no problem with spelling.*

2 Write these sentences, putting *anything* or *nothing* in the gaps:

a *I don't want ______ to do with it.*

b *Unfortunately, there's no way we can do ______ about it.*

c *There was ______ anyone could do.*

d *If you don't need ______ else then go away!*

Order in sentences

Sentence work

- To revise ordering of phrases and clauses within sentences

The order we use words in a sentence is as important for meaning as the actual words we use.

Spelling Bee just told Milo that he could spell anything.

Spelling Bee told just Milo that he could spell anything.

1 a What is the difference in meaning between the two sentences in the box?

b Write the sentence in the box, moving the **just** to another position that still makes sense.

2 Copy these sentences, then underline the phrase that is in the wrong position. Write each sentence again, correctly. The first is done for you.

a *Milo put Tock when he misbehaved in the kennel.*
Milo put Tock in the kennel when he misbehaved.

b *They saw Spelling Bee in the marketplace which was buzzing.*

c *We know a man who lives in a house with a loud voice.*

d *The bee sat on the wagon with flapping wings.*

Tip

Phrases and clauses that describe something should be as near as possible to what they are describing.

Word work

- To revise some key rules for adding suffixes

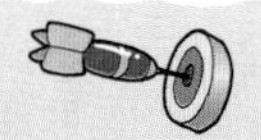

Remember

All rules have exceptions e.g. true/truly; argue/argument.

Adding suffixes to words ending in *e*

Remember, when adding suffixes to most words ending in **e**:

- drop the **e** if the suffix begins with a vowel letter or is **y**

  wake + ing = waking

- keep the **e** if the suffix begins with a consonant

  wake + ful = wakeful

1 a Add *ing* to: *hide take make strive slope hope shave bite*

b Add *able* to: *use value believe cure recognise love*

2 a Add *ly* to: *close lame like fine wise brave safe*

b Add *ful* to: *grace hope shame care waste*

Word work

- To consider the use of dialogue words other than *said*

Using synonyms for said

"I knew you'd like it," laughed the letter man.

"All of them aren't so good," he confided.

The careful choice and use of words improves our writing. Here is a list of some of the many words which can be used as synonyms for **said**:

insisted bellowed answered shouted warned asked enquired yelled laughed squealed cried growled sobbed remarked urged decided muttered whispered explained continued pleaded called confided replied interrupted whimpered

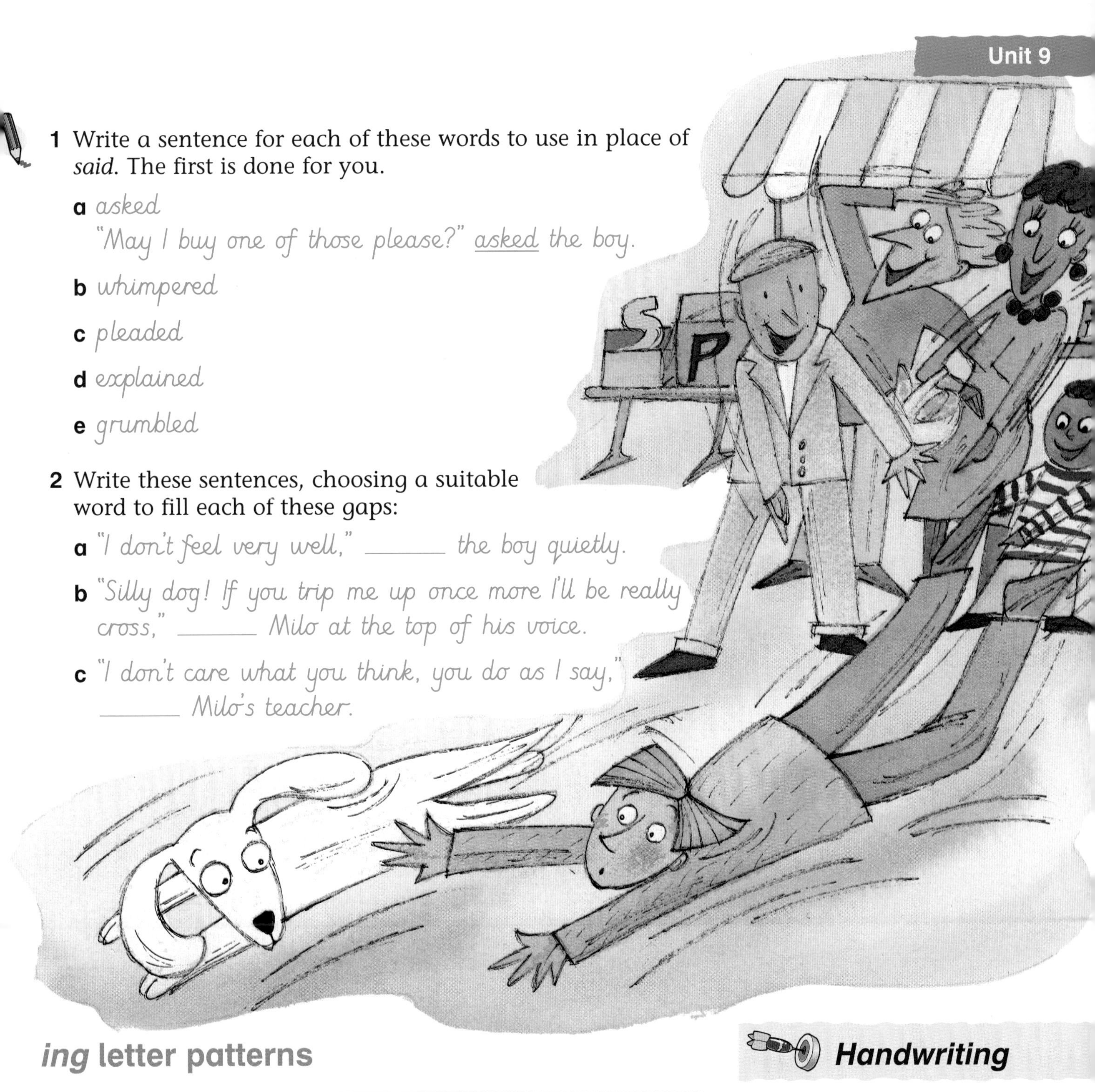

1 Write a sentence for each of these words to use in place of *said*. The first is done for you.

a *asked*
"May I buy one of those please?" asked the boy.

b *whimpered*

c *pleaded*

d *explained*

e *grumbled*

2 Write these sentences, choosing a suitable word to fill each of these gaps:

a *"I don't feel very well," ______ the boy quietly.*

b *"Silly dog! If you trip me up once more I'll be really cross," ______ Milo at the top of his voice.*

c *"I don't care what you think, you do as I say," ______ Milo's teacher.*

ing letter patterns

Handwriting

ping king ting ying ping king ting ying

1 a Practise the letter patterns three times.

b Write these words neatly across your page:
hoping taking wasting worrying

2 a Under each of the words, list as many other words as you can that end with the same letter string.

b Use the words in your lists to write a short poem or limerick.

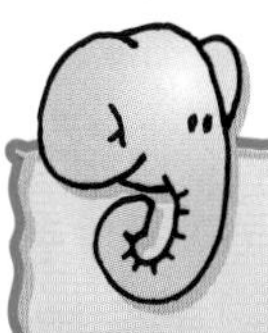

Remember

A limerick is a funny poem of five lines.

Hidden Pollution

Sentence work

- To consider some forms of official language

Official language

The owner of this vehicle is hereby informed that its exhaust system is permitting too many noxious fumes to escape into the atmosphere. It may not be driven on public roads until a new exhaust is fitted.

Written language like this is found on official forms and documents.

- It is *impersonal* writing – it doesn't refer to people by name or by using personal pronouns and other words, like *you we* or *our*.
- It uses formal words, like *hereby*, and passive sentences.
- It makes statements and demands, and is *not very friendly*.

Remember

Personal pronouns include **I, you, we, they.**

1 Write these sentences making the style more formal. The first is done for you.

a We would be very pleased if you would not light your bonfires on hot days.

Bonfires may not be lit on hot days.

b Our staff from the council are visiting your area to make sure you are taking notice of this regulation.

c We would like lorry drivers stuck in traffic jams in the tunnel to turn off their vehicle's engine.

d We are writing to let you know that you now live in a smokeless zone.

2 Write these phrases that are often found on formal documents in another way:

a notice is hereby served

b forms may be obtained from

c notwithstanding the present situation

d further to your recent correspondence

e those wishing to attend the public hearing

Writing shorter versions

Sentence work

- To practise summary writing

Some pollution is more easily spotted than others, but smoke and fumes, which are not very visible, are serious problems. They cause acid rain that kills trees, and smog and particulates that affect people's health, and some fumes seriously damage the Earth's atmosphere.

This is a **summary** of the information in the passage *Hidden Pollution* that is about hidden dangers.

We sometimes need to write a **short version** of a paragraph or article. A summary should be short, but it should contain all the main points.

1 Write a summary of the information below under the heading Pollution Kills, which is from the passage *Hidden Pollution*.

Pollution kills!

Over the last fifty years, pollution has become one of the most serious problems facing our world. It chokes rivers, smothers life in the oceans, damages the soil and poisons the air.

Pollution is the presence in the environment of large quantities of dangerous chemicals, many created by people, that can harm life and cause long-lasting damage to our planet.

Remember

A good summary will contain all the key information.

2 Choose an information book on a subject that interests you. Find a page or section with about 400 words. Write a summary of the information in the passage, using no more than 150 words.

Word work

- To practise the rule for adding suffixes to words ending with *y*

Adding suffixes to words ending with *y*

Remember, to add ***ing*** when a word ends with ***y***, just add it!

try trying

But, to add any other suffixes, first change the ***y*** to ***i*** before adding the suffix.

try tried   messy messily

1 a Add ing and ed to each of these words:

spy fry dry cry marry hurry worry

b Write the words in 1a as plural nouns or as singular verbs, like this:

spy spies

Remember

Singular verbs often end in ***s*** or ***es***.

2 a Add ly to each of these words, and write the new words:

happy	funny
sloppy	merry
easy	noisy

b Use two of your new words in a sentence.

Word work

- To develop argument vocabulary

Words for arguments

There are several useful words we can use when writing a sensible, balanced argument.

I firmly believe that there should be more control over pollution. *Although* we all need transport, *in my opinion* not enough care is taken to minimise diesel fumes. *Furthermore*, those who cause the pollution should be responsible for paying to have it removed.

1 Use some of the words in the box in a short argument that explains your opinions about whether, in a free country, people should be allowed to drop litter anywhere they please.

believe opinion whereas besides although furthermore consequently conclusion

Helpful words

thoughtless disgusting environment messy unpleasant civilised consequences dangerous

2 Next to each of these words write a definition. Use a dictionary to help you.

a argument
b discussion
c viewpoint
d contention
e opinion
f conclusion

ly and *ily* suffixes

Handwriting

ly ily ly ily ly ily ly ily ly ily ly ily ly ily ly ily ly ily

1 **a** Practise the letter patterns three times.

b Neatly copy these words twice each:

silly chilly billy hilly

happily merrily shiftily noisily

2 **a** Neatly copy this nonsense sentence:

The old billy looked at me shiftily, so I ran swiftly and noisily along the hilly, chilly farm track.

b Make your own sentence that includes as many words as possible ending in ly.

Unit 11

The Midnight Fox

Sentence work

- To practise adjective phrases and introduce adverb phrases

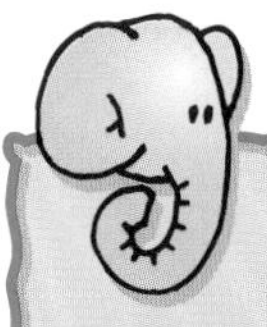

Remember

An **adjective** gives more information about a noun; an **adverb** gives more information about a verb.

Tip

Notice how commas are used to give a slight pause when using some phrases.

Adjective and adverb phrases

Sometimes we need to write a phrase rather than just a single adjective or adverb.

The black fox, light and free as the wind, was by the creek.

This phrase tells us more about the noun, the **fox**. It is an adjective phrase.

She came leaping across the green, green grass.

This phrase tells us more about the verb, **leaping**. It is an adverb phrase.

1 Copy these sentences, adding an adjective phrase to complete each one. Underline the noun being described.

a *The night, ______, reminded me of the night I shall always remember.*

b *I lay in my bed, ______, thinking back five years.*

c *______, the fox comes running towards me.*

d *I see the oak tree, ______, and feel the rain beating against me.*

Helpful adjective phrases

soft and warm
massive and gnarled
dark and stormy
Black and carefree

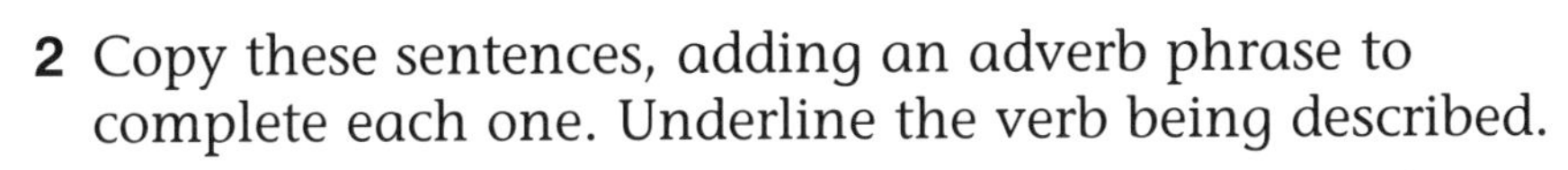

2 Copy these sentences, adding an adverb phrase to complete each one. Underline the verb being described.

a ______ *the rain beats against my window.*

b *I sleep,* ______, *thinking about that night.*

c *I seem to hear,* ______, *the bark of the midnight fox.*

d *My Mom told me* ______ *that I was going to Aunt Millie's farm.*

Punctuation practice

1 Copy these sentences, adding the capital letters and missing punctuation at the end of each one:

a *have you ever had a frightening experience*

b *crash*

c *what was that*

d *i hate storms when i am in bed*

e *it was soon quiet again*

2 Copy these sentences, adding the capital letters and missing punctuation, including commas and apostrophes:

a *mom says im silly to worry but i cant help it*

b *its easy for her to say that shes not my age*

c *she doesnt know how much i hate lightning*

d *i remembered that night in august at aunt millies farm*

e *i dont like staying with old relatives do you*

Remember

Adverbs and adverb phrases tell us **how**, **when** and **where** the action of a verb is happening.

Helpful adverb phrases

in an excited way
plainly as I heard that August night,
fitfully and uneasily
Sometimes at night

Sentence work

- To revise the end of sentence punctuation marks, commas and apostrophes

Remember

Use **.** or **?** or **!** for the end of each sentence.

Word work

- To revise the rule for adding prefixes to root words

Tip

When adding a prefix, whatever the last letter of the prefix or the first letter of the word, don't be tempted to leave off any letters!

Adding prefixes

If you need to add a prefix to a word, the spelling rule is easy: Just add it!

dis + appearing = disappearing

dis + satisfied = di<u>ss</u>atisfied (NOT disatisfied)

1 a Add the prefix *un* to each of these words:

tidy necessary natural invited named numbered

b Add the prefix *dis* to each of these words:

similar appear satisfy trust obey organise

c Add the prefix *im* to each of these words:

modest movable mortal possible moral measurable

2 Use a dictionary to help you find as many words as possible that begin with the prefix ***over***.

Borrowed words

I was just taking off the cellophane when my mom came in.

Although *cellophane* is a word made up quite recently by the people who invented the thin plastic covering, most words in English with ***ph*** came originally from the Greek language:

phone Greek for sound or voice
photo Greek for light
s**ph**ere Greek for ball
gra**ph** Greek for writing

1 Sort these words into four lists according to their Greek meaning:

telegraph saxophone paragraph hemisphere graph
telephone photographic atmospheric microphone
spherical autograph photocopier

2 a Add any other words you can to each of the four groups. A dictionary may be helpful.

b Using the information in the box, write your own definition for three of the words.

Word work

- To realise that other languages have influenced English

Special patterns with prefixes

unn diss imm unn diss imm unn diss imm

1 a Practise the letter patterns three times.

b Neatly copy these tricky words twice each:
unnecessary unnatural unnamed
dissimilar dissatisfy
immodest immovable immeasurable

2 Neatly write three sentences, one of each to include a word beginning unn, diss and imm.

Handwriting

Joining the Library

Sentence work

- To consider how some verbs can change their meaning

Changing verb meanings

put out *put off* *put up* *put back* *put upon*

The meaning of several important verbs changes according to the word linked to them.

She was put off the book by the boring cover.

1 Use each of these in short sentences to show what they mean:

a make-up **b** make out

c make over **d** make for

e make off **f** make do

Helpful words

in out over of
to about off

2 Make as many different verbs as possible based on each of these common verbs by adding different prepositions or adverbs:

a take **b** get

c talk **d** run

Abbreviations

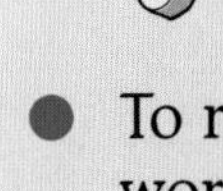

Sentence work

- To revise abbreviated words

In a questionnaire, where there may not be much space, words are sometimes abbreviated.

Telephone number
Tel No: ___________________

Age ___________ Date of birth
D of B: _______________

Tip

Abbreviated means shortened.

1 How might you abbreviate these?

a British Broadcasting Corporation

b Member of Parliament

c European Union

d United States of America

e Prime Minister

f doctor

g mister

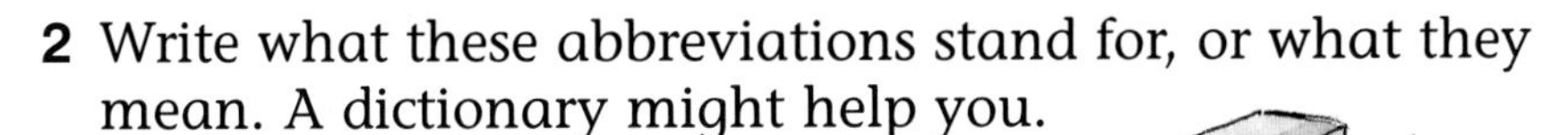

2 Write what these abbreviations stand for, or what they mean. A dictionary might help you.

a RSPCA **b** ITV

c e.g. **d** a.m.

e PS **f** PC

g IOU **h** UN

i etc. **j** PTO

Helpful words

please turn over
and so on (et cetera)
personal computer
United Nations
Royal Society for the Prevention of Cruelty to Animals
postscript (extra thought)
morning (ante meridiem)
I owe you
for example (exempli gratia)
Independent Television

Word work

- To practise alphabetical ordering skills

Remember

The books are arranged by the author's surname, or family name.

Using alphabetical order

In a library we need to be able to use alphabetical ordering skills.

- Dictionaries and most encyclopedias have words and information arranged in alphabetical order.
- Fiction books are arranged on the shelves according to the surname of the author.

1 On the spines of these encylopedias are the initial letters of the subjects they have information about.

Write the number of the volume in which you would find out about:

a space travel
b railways
c birds
d Germany
e pollution
f snow
g lions
h oxygen
i Elizabeth II
j whales

2 Write these authors' names in the order in which you would expect to find their books on the shelves:

a Lewis Carroll   Joan Aitken   Enid Blyton   Roald Dahl

b David Kynoch   Betsy Byars   Richard Parker
C. S. Lewis   Rukshana Smith   Forrest Wilson

c Nirupa Mukherjee   John Miles   Maggie Moore
Jill Murphy

Word origins

Dictionaries have more about where the words that we now use originally came from.

bait *n* something edible fixed to a hook or in a trap to attract fish or animals [C13: from ON *beita* to hunt]

noun *13th century* *Old Norse* (early Scandinavian language)

1 Use a dictionary to help you discover as much as you can about the origins of these words, especially which language they came from, what they meant in that language and when they started being used in English:

a convoy
b banquet
c atmosphere
d thesaurus
e diary
f mathematics
g marathon
h piano

2 Choose three words from question 1 to put in sentences to demonstrate their modern use.

Practising capitals

I L T E F H A K M N V W X Y Z

1 Neatly copy the capital letters in the box. None of them has a curve.

2 **a** Copy these silly sentences:

WILLIAM TELL FELL IN THE WELL.

WHAT A YELL!

LET HIM YELL.

LET WILLIAM TELL YELL IN THE WELL!

b Write some of your own sentences using only capital letters without curves.

Word work

- To discover how dictionaries often give information about word origins

Tip

In a dictionary you may find:
n = noun
v = verb
adj = adjective
adv = adverb
prep = preposition
c = century
O= Old
M = Middle
E = English
F = French
N = Norse (from Scandinavia)
L = Latin (from Italy)
Gk = Greek (from Greece)

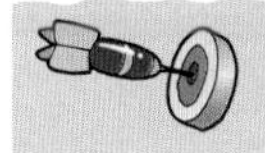

Handwriting

Tip

Make all your letters the same height.

Draw a faint guideline to help you.

Kidnapped

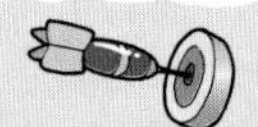

Sentence work

- To revise abstract nouns

Making abstract nouns

there came on me a deadly sickness

Remember, while most nouns are things we can see or touch, **abstract nouns** are names we give to qualities or ideas.

Most abstract nouns are made from other words:

sick **sickness**   thief **theft**   improve **improvement**

1 Copy and finish these statements with an abstract noun. The first is done for you.

a To encourage a person is to give them encouragement.

b To hate someone is to be guilty of ______.

c To please a parent is to give them ______.

d To grieve is to feel a sense of ______.

e To agree about something is to reach an ______.

f To entertain parents and friends is to put on some ______.

Helpful words

grief hatred pleasure entertainment agreement

2 Write the abstract noun that is related to each of these words by adding a suffix:

a dark	**b** lazy	**c** happy
d arrange	**e** treat	**f** involve
g king	**h** free	**i** wise
j post	**k** pack	**l** stupid
m observe	**n** invite	**o** inform

Helpful suffixes for abstract nouns

ness ment dom age hood ion ity

Using commas in long sentences

Commas that tell the reader where to make a slight pause, make reading longer sentences easier.

So there we stood, side by side upon a small rock slippery with spray, a far broader leap in front of us, and the river dinning upon all sides.

Sentence work

- To use commas to mark pauses in sentences

1 Copy this sentence neatly, and, without looking at the passage in the Comprehension and Writing Skills book, add the missing commas:

Then putting his hands to his mouth and his mouth to my ear he shouted "Hang or drown!" and turning his back upon me leaped over the farther branch of the stream and landed safe.

2 Copy these sentences neatly, and add the missing commas:

I bent low on my knees and flung myself forth with the kind of anger of despair that has sometimes stood me in stead of courage. Sure enough it was but my hands that reached the full length; these slipped caught again slipped again; and I was sliddering back into the lynn when Alan seized me first by the hair then by the collar and with a great strain dragged me into safety.

Word work

- To practise the *sure* and *ture* spelling patterns

Tip

Most words ending in ***ure*** are abstract nouns.

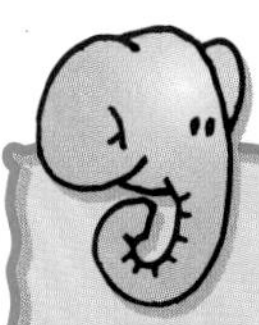

Remember

Some words are changed slightly when a suffix is added.

sure and *ture* spelling patterns

The ***ure*** suffix usually follows the letter ***s*** or ***t***, depending on the spelling of the root word to which it is added.

plea*sure* depar*ture*

1 Write the ***ure*** word that is related to each of these words:

a moist **b** expose
c please **d** enclose
e fail **f** press

2 Look at the words in the box. Each has a *family* word which has a ***ure*** suffix or ending. Write the words and next to each write the related word, like this:

natural = nature

natural	furnish	pictorial	captivate
torturing	security	insurance	agricultural

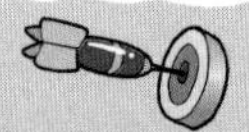

Word work

- To demonstrate how word meanings change over time

Changing words and phrases

I bent low on my knees and flung myself forth.

We would not use this sentence if we were speaking today. Over the years, words and phrases change.

1 Copy this table. Write a brief definition of each word as used today.

Word	Original meaning	Today's meaning
nice	silly	
flat	level surface	
keen	sharp	
wicked	evil	
cool	not very warm	
trainer	person who trains others	

Remember

Definition means *meaning.*

Tip

Some of these words are still used for their original meaning as well as their new meaning.

2 These phrases and sentences are from *Kidnapped*. Write them as we might say them today.

a the river dinning upon all sides

b leaped over the farther branch of the stream, and landed safe

c I had just wit enough to see

d I bent low on my knees and flung myself forth

e I was sliddering back into the lynn

f I had a stitch that came near to overmaster me

sure and *ture* letter patterns and suffixes

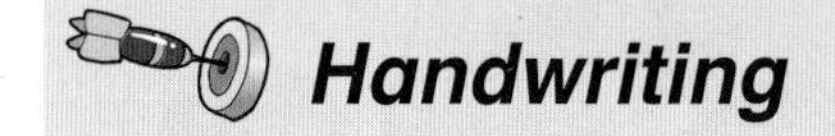

Handwriting

sure ture sure ture sure ture sure ture sure ture sure ture

1 **a** Practise the letter patterns three times.

b Neatly copy these words twice each:

fracture adventure moisture puncture
dentures treasure pleasure leisure

2 Neatly write a ***sure*** or ***ture*** word to answer each clue:

a a split tyre
b broken bone
c a relaxing time
d dampness
e hidden valuables
f set of false teeth

Tip

Look back at the words in question 1 to help you.

An Equal Chance

Sentence work

- To consider some of the reasons for editing sentences

Tip

Omissions are things left out.

Editing

When we draft a piece of writing, it is important to read it again to correct and improve it.
Look for:

- spelling mistakes
- punctuation errors or omissions
- unnecessary words
- using better words
- the order of words and phrases
- double negatives
- adding more detail

1 Write these sentences, correcting spelling and punctuation, and omitting any unnecessary words:

a *Some children can be very extremly unkind to some other children just becuse the other children they know and they are being unkind to are different in some way or another way*

b *It is usully normally a good thing to right a letter to your MP or to someone or to your councilor or someone if you think there is discriminaton going on in your area or anywhere else and say to them that you think discriminaton is a very very bad thing to be happning*

2 In these sentences, use a better word or words than those underlined, remove any double negatives and add a further phrase to give more detail (where you see this mark ⋏):

a *Nelson Mandela was a <u>good</u> leader of South Africa.*

b *There wasn't nothing ⋏ could do to stop the fight.*

c *Discrimination ⋏ should be stopped.*

d *People who bully are <u>bad</u>.*

e *It needs courage ⋏ to stop bullying.*

Using apostrophes

Sentence work

- To revise apostrophes for contraction and possession

Remember, apostrophes are used:
- for contractions
- for possessive nouns.

A **contraction** is made by leaving out some letters and putting an **apostrophe** (') in their place:

what's is a contraction for *what is*

When something belongs to someone we use an apostrophe (') and an **s**, like this ***'s***:

the *girl's* problem

girl's is called a **possessive noun**.

For plurals of nouns, like girls, we must put an apostrophe *after* the **s**.

three *girls'* problems

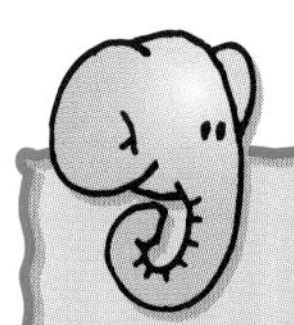

Remember

The **apostrophe** shows where letters have been left out.

1 a Write a contraction for each of these:

it will she is would not has not we shall
do not you are I will they are could not

b Copy and add the apostrophe in each of these:

my Dads bike the two boys bags
the womens hairdresser Asmats lunchbox
our neighbours dog

2 Copy these sentences and add the missing apostrophes:

a Theyre coming to collect Mums present.

b We cant find Dads scarf or my two brothers hats.

c Its a pity I lost its lid.

d Our teams playing at home tonight.

e "Rights right," said Ben.

f Someones been very unkind!

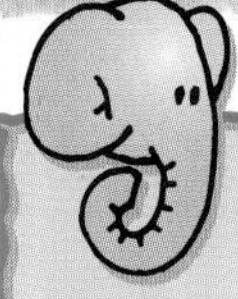

Remember

Its is possessive; **it's** is a contraction of *it is*.

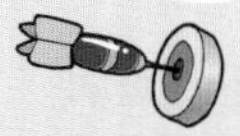

Word work

- To realise how mnemonics can help with the spelling of tricky words

Tip

Mnemonic comes from the Greek word to remember.

Tip

The best mnemonics are the ones you make up for yourself.

Mnemonics

Mnemonics can help us to remember how to spell tricky words.

Necessary is a smelly word – it has a cess pit in the middle of it.

If you remember that, you'll never again worry about whether necessary has one or two c's or s's!

1 Copy these words and mnemonics. Underline the part each mnemonic helps us to remember:

a *library* — *no brats allowed in this library*

b *bicycle* — *you'll slip off your bicycle on icy roads*

c *brought* — *brought means to bring*

d *bought* — *bought means to buy*

e *chocolate* — *you're too late for any chocolate*

f *friend* — *make up with your friend on a Friday*

2 Make up your own mnemonics for these tricky words, or choose six others that you especially want to remember:

a ignorant **b** obedient

c thermometer **d** encyclopedia

e occasion **f** parallel

English prefixes

befriend **over**take **out**burst

Most prefixes originally came to English from other languages, such as Greek or Latin, but some are English words and are therefore easier to spell and remember.

1 Write four words that begin with each of these prefixes:

a *be* **b** *up*
c *to* **d** *over*
e *under* **f** *out*

2 Write a short definition of each of these words:

a *forbid* **b** *forlorn*
c *forsake* **d** *forecast*
e *forefathers* **f** *foresight*

Practising capitals

B C D G J O P Q R S U

1 Neatly copy the capital letters in the box. Each of them has a curve.

2 **a** Write five words in capital letters, using only the letters in the box.

b Make up five words using just these letters, and next to each write a definition, like this:

DOGBUS – a vehicle for carrying dogs

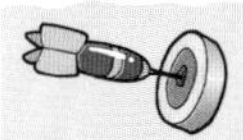

Word work

- To consider some prefixes with an English origin

Tip

Use a dictionary to help if you can't think of enough words, or you need help with some definitions.

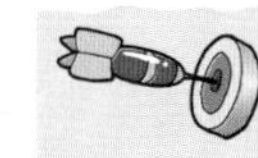

Handwriting

Tip

Make all your letters the same height.

Draw a faint guideline to help you.

Unit 15

The Wind

Sentence work

- To revise the structure of the present and future tenses

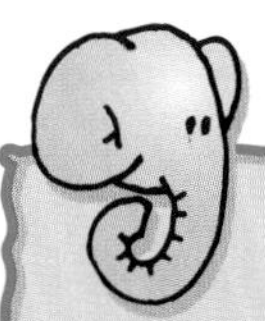

Remember

The **present tense** tells us what is happening now.

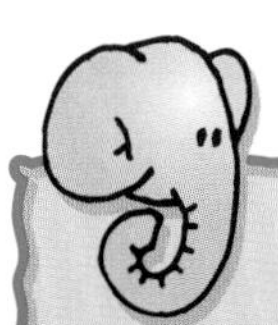

Remember

The **future tense** tells us what will, or should, happen in the future.

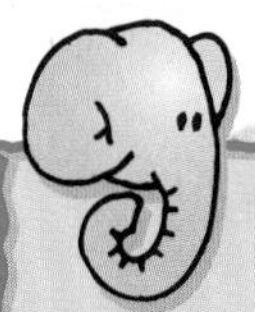

Remember

Helper verbs are sometimes called **auxiliary** verbs.

Present and future tenses

We make the **present tense** by simply using the verb family name:

The wind *blows*.

or by using a helper verb and adding the suffix ***ing***:

It *is blowing* hard.

We make the **future tense** by using the verb family name with a helper verb:

The forecast says the wind *will blow* tomorrow.

1 Copy this table, filling in the gaps.

Verb family	Present tense	Future tense
to howl	it howls it is howling	it will howl
to worry	she _____ she _____ _____	she _____ _____
to run	he _____ he _____ _____	he _____ _____
to cry	they _____ they _____ _____	they _____ _____
to rain	it _____ it _____ _____	it _____ _____

2 Write these sentences in the present tense, using helper verbs where necessary:

a *The wind blew hard.*

b *We held tight to the railings.*

c *I tried not to fall over.*

d *Some tiles came off the roof.*

e *The tiles fell on a car.*

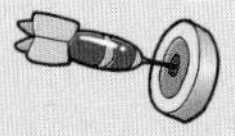

Sentence work

- To introduce personal and impersonal writing

Tip

Personal writing often has pronouns like **I**, **we**; impersonal writing often has the pronoun **it**.

Personal and impersonal writing

In **personal** writing, the author writes as if he or she or a particular person is involved.

We saw the wind blow down a huge tree.

This is a **personal** statement.

In **impersonal** writing, the author writes in general terms.

The wind caused considerable damage.

This is an **impersonal** statement.

1 Change these sentences from personal to impersonal:

a I saw the tree blown over and crush the car.

b We were pleased that no one was in the car.

c The next thing we knew was that the fire and rescue services were rushing to the scene.

d I said to them that no one was hurt.

2 Change these sentences from impersonal to personal:

a It is surprising how much damage the storm caused.

b Several houses had roof damage.

c Some people had to spend a night in the school hall.

d It is not expected to be as windy tomorrow.

Making nouns plural

Word work

- To revise the main rules for making nouns plural

Remember, we need to look at the letters at the end of a noun before deciding how to make it plural.

- Simply add ***s*** to most words.
- Add ***es*** to most words that end in *s*, *x*, *sh* and *ch*.
- Add ***es*** to most words that end in *o*, except for words ending in *oo*, music words, or shortened words.
- For most words ending in *y*, change the *y* to ***i*** and then add ***es***.

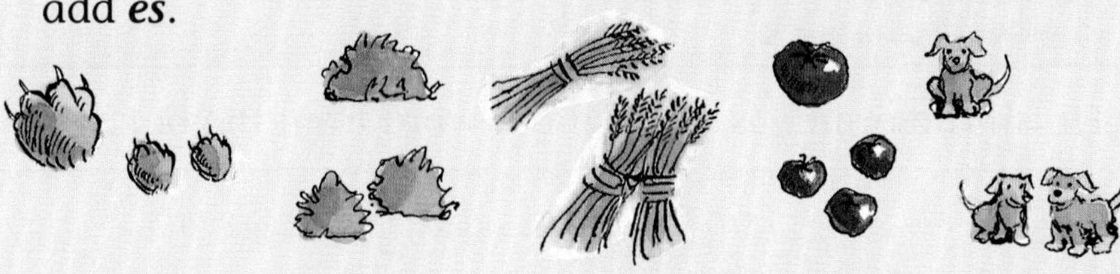

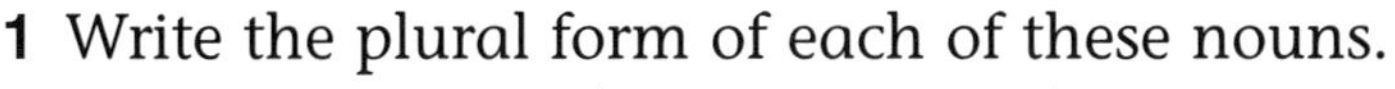

1 Write the plural form of each of these nouns.

a motto **b** turkey **c** cockatoo **d** country
e window **f** piano **g** church **h** box
i photo **j** play **k** fly **l** igloo
m donkey **n** nursery **o** activity **p** potato

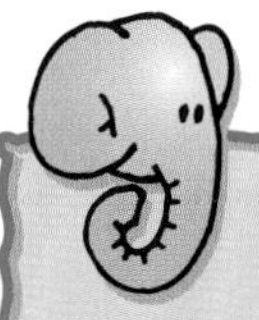

Remember

If a word has a vowel letter before the ***y***, just add ***s***, e.g. *tray trays*.

2 Copy and complete this table.

Singular nouns	Plural nouns
glass	
	trees
cello	
daisy	
	potatoes
watch	
	berries
dish	
leaf	
donkey	
	volcanoes

Word work

- To revise metaphors and similes

Special expressions that describe

Metaphors are where the writer writes about something as if it were something else.

The wind is a wolf
That sniffs at doors
And rattles windows
With his paws.

Similes are where the writer compares something with something else.

The wind blew as fast as an express train.

Tip

Metaphors and **similes** are expressions that suggest different things are in some ways similar.

Tip

Similes always start with **like** or **as**.

1 Finish these similes, choosing a word from the box.

razor swan picture daisy bee soot

a as graceful as a ______

b as fresh as a ______

c as busy as a ______

d as sharp as a ______

e as black as ______

f as pretty as a ______

2 Write sentences that explain what each of these expressions mean:

a The storm is an angry giant.

b The snow is a thick, white blanket.

c The hare ran like the wind.

d The sky was on fire.

es and *ies* patterns

es ies es ies es ies es ies es ies es ies es ies es ies

1 a Practise the letter patterns three times.

b Neatly copy these words twice each:

glasses bushes boxes churches
berries cherries daisies puppies

2 a Neatly copy the silly sentence:

Foxes chase the puppies eating berries off the bushes in the daisies.

b Make your own silly sentence that includes as many plural nouns as possible.

Unit 16

A Question of Marriage

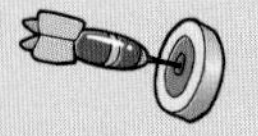

Sentence work

- To revise proverbs

Proverbs

Most countries and cultures have their **proverbs**. This is a Swahili proverb from Africa. A dhow is a sailing ship.

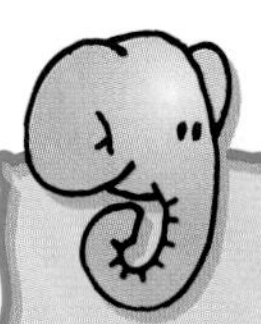

Remember

Proverbs are short, wise sayings which are used to teach a simple lesson. Many have been handed down from generation to generation.

1 Match each of these British proverbs with an ending from the box below:

A friend in need ...

Birds of a feather ...

The early bird ...

Least said ...

soonest mended	*catches the worm*
is a friend indeed	*flock together*

2 **a** Write a sentence to explain the lesson each of these Swahili proverbs is teaching:

Potter! Knead your clay while it is wet.

The miser's money will be eaten by the cockroaches.

The man who gave up did not become rich.

b Write a short story that uses the proverb 'A man alone cannot push a dhow into the sea'.

Sentence work

- To practise punctuating dialogue

Practising punctuation

1 Here is an extract from *A Question of Marriage*. Copy it, and without looking at the passage, add the missing speech marks and commas.

And what is a camel's pen? asked the young man.

That's rather a silly question giggled the beautiful sister. It's a high fence that keeps the camels in at night.

I see said the young man. And now can you tell me what is the best sauce to eat with boiled millet?

Of course I can said the beautiful sister without thinking. The best sauce to serve with millet is melted ghee and milk.

Thank you said the young man.

2 Here is another extract from *A Question of Marriage*. Copy it, and without looking at the passage, add the missing speech marks and commas, and also decide when a different person speaks, so that you begin a new line.

Tell me he said what is the best blanket a man can sleep on? Peace of mind said the plain girl for without peace of mind no one can sleep a wink. What is a camel's pen? asked the young man. A camel's pen is man himself, for it is man who herds the camels together for safety at night.

Word work

- To revise some key rules for adding suffixes

Some rules for adding suffixes

- When adding suffixes to most words ending in ***e*** we drop the ***e*** before adding a suffix that begins with a vowel letter, *but* if the word ends in ***ce*** or ***ge*** keep the ***e*** for the suffixes ***able*** or ***ous***:

  noti**ce** noticeable
- If you are unsure about whether to use the suffix ***able*** or ***ible***, remember many more words use the suffix ***able*** than ***ible***:

  enjoy enjoy**able**

1 Choose one suffix from the box to add to each of these root words.

ing ion ment ous able ary

a fame	**b** enjoy
c imagine	**d** improve
e operate	**f** excite
g smile	**h** outrage
i develop	**j** invent
k leave	**l** place

2 Add able or ible to each of these roots. Write them in two lists. Check your answers in a dictionary. Which is the longer list?

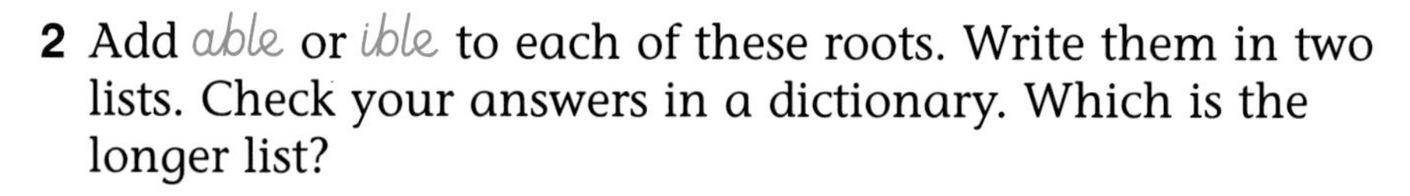
miser defence value agree sense perish response cure
force advise notice honour contempt depend reason

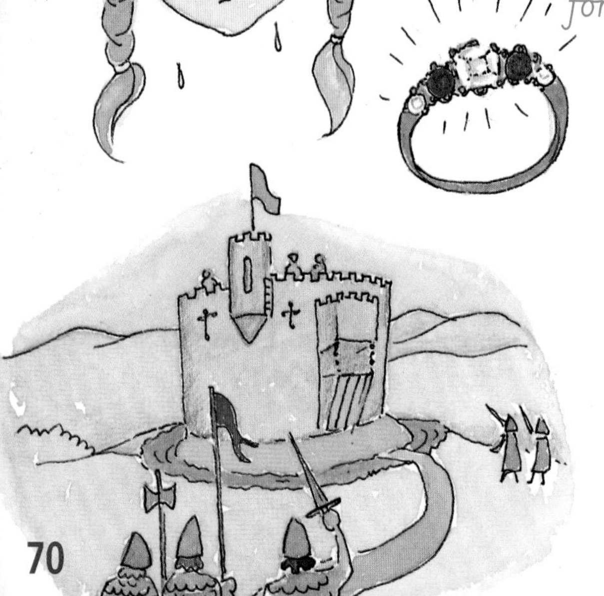

Word riddles

Word work

- To find hidden words in letter sequences

1 Each of these letter strings contains two words which are illustrated in the picture. The letters are in the correct order, but are mixed together. The first one is done for you.

a vhilulatges
village huts

b capmeelsn

c gliriaoffnes

d heilppeoppothaamnuts

Helpful words

elephant giraffe hippopotamus pen lions camels

2 Make up some similar riddles to give to your friends.

ous and *ious* letter patterns and suffixes

Handwriting

ous ious ous ious ous ious ous ious ous ious ous ious

1 **a** Practise the letter patterns three times.

b Neatly copy these words twice each:

famous nervous jealous enormous
various previous curious serious

2 Neatly write four more words to add to the ***ous*** words and four more to add to the ***ious*** patterns.

Unit 17

A New Home

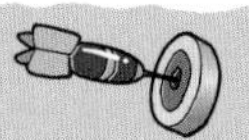

Sentence work

- To revise the structure of the present and past tenses

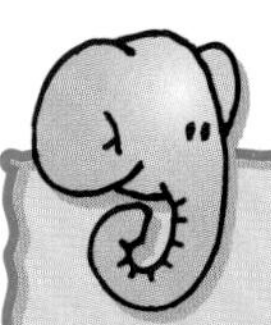

Remember

The **past** tense tells us what has already happened.

Tip

Most **fictional stories** and **reports** are written in the past tense.

Helpful words

brought felt
went saw
came

Present and past tenses

We usually make the **past tense** by simply adding ***d*** or ***ed*** to the verb family name:

When she opened her eyes in the morning …

or

When she had opened her eyes in the morning …

or by using *was* or *were* and adding the suffix ***ing***:

She was opening her eyes when …

Some verbs have **irregular past tenses** and use a slightly different spelling from the family name:

The housemaid came in and lit the fire.

1 a Copy this table, filling in the gaps.

Verb	Past tenses
to open	she opened she had opened she was opening
to hear	
to live	
to stay	
to dress	

b Copy this table, filling in the gaps.

Verb	Irregular past tense
to come	she came she had come she was coming
to feel	
to see	
to bring	
to go	

2 Write these sentences in the past tense. Underline the words you have needed to change.

a *She has come into the room.*

b *The maid kneels on the rug.*

c *Mary lies and watches her.*

d *She thinks the room is gloomy.*

e *Out of the window she can see a stretch of land.*

f *"What is that?" she says.*

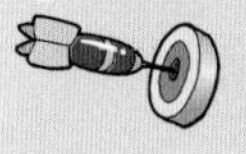

Sentence work

- To revise the use of capital letters

Using capital letters

Remember, capital letters are used:

- to begin sentences
- for proper nouns
- for the small word **I** (and **I**'m **I**'ve **I**'ll)
- for the first word and other important words in a title

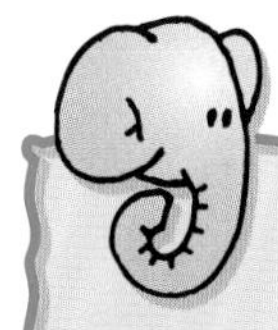

Remember

Proper nouns are actual names of people, pets, places etc.

1 Copy the words in this list correctly that need a capital letter:

heidi switzerland country ursula england
i mary we peter martha birmingham the
pennine hills river thames stream atlantic ocean

2 Write these sentences correctly:

a *the story of heidi was written by johanna spyri.*

b *heidi lives in switzerland with her grandfather.*

c *the goats were looked after by peter.*

d *"can i help get topsy and dusky from their stalls?" heidi asked her grandfather.*

e *frances hodgson burnett wrote a famous book called the secret garden.*

f *it is about a girl called mary who moves from india to live in england.*

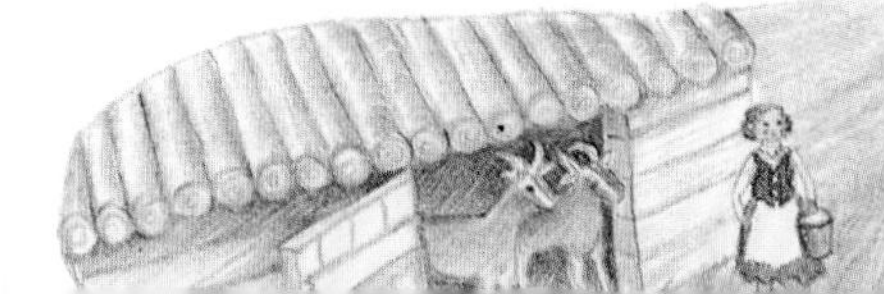

Word work

- To practise spelling words with unstressed vowels

Unstressed vowels

Say these words aloud:

mountain different

When these words are said aloud, the letters underlined are hard to hear. Remember, they are called **unstressed** vowels, and are sometimes forgotten when the words are written.

1 Copy these words. Circle the unstressed vowels.

a *separate* **b** *business*
c *miserable* **d** *favourite*
e *sentence* **f** *necessary*
g *January* **h** *jewellery*
i *sufficient* **j** *essentially*
k *torrential* **l** *delicious*

2 Use a dictionary to help you spot the unstressed vowels that have been left out of these words. Copy the correct spellings.

a *vegtables* **b** *intresting*
c *happning* **d** *dictionry*
e *temprature* **f** *memry*
g *machinry* **h** *impatent*

Word work

- To revise vowel and consonant letters

What's missing?

Remember, the **vowel letters** are ***a***, ***e***, ***i***, ***o***, ***u***. Sometimes the letter ***y*** acts as a vowel in short words where it sounds like *i*, such as in *by* and *try*.
All the other letters are called **consonants**.

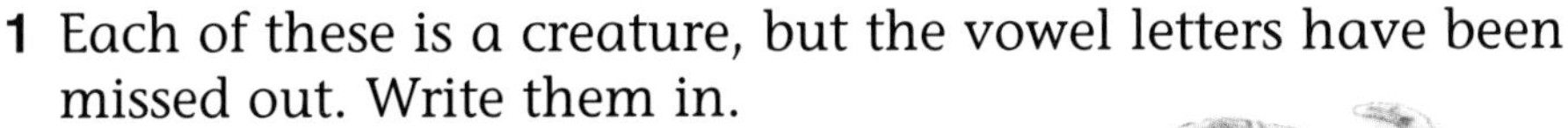

1 Each of these is a creature, but the vowel letters have been missed out. Write them in.

a b_ll
b sn_k_
c d_ng_
d _l_ph_nt
e z_br_
f sh__p
g r__k
h r_b_n

2 Each of these is a country, but some of the consonant letters have been missed out. Write them in.

a S_i_ze__a_d
b En__a_d
c I_e_an_
d _a_es
e S_o__a_d

Helpful words

Switzerland
Wales
Scotland
Ireland
England

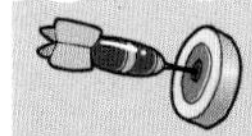

Handwriting

ary, *ery* and *ory* letter patterns

ary ery ory ary ery ory ary ery ory ary ery ory

1 a Practise the letter patterns three times.

b Neatly copy these three lists of words:

primary library burglary

bravery mystery nursery

history victory memory

2 a Neatly add another two words to each of the three lists.

b Write one sentence for each list in which you include three of the words that you have written.

Dangers in a Victorian Factory

Sentence work

- To revise the use of comparing words

Making comparisons

Adjectives describe nouns. We often add ***er*** or ***est*** to adjectives if we want to compare nouns:

Factories are safer today than in Victorian times.

noun *comparing adjective*

Adverbs describe verbs. In the same way as we add ***er*** or ***est*** to adjectives, we can add these suffixes to adverbs to compare verbs:

People in factories worked longer than they do today.

verb *comparing adverb*

If the adjective or adverb is a longer word, then instead of adding ***er*** or ***est*** we usually write **more** or **most**, or **less** or **least** in front of it.

1 Copy and finish this table of comparing words and phrases.

fast	faster	fastest
heavy	heavier	
risky		
deep		
late		
cheeky		

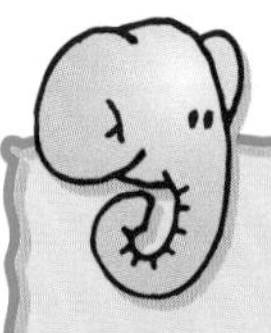

Remember

To add ***er*** or ***est*** to a word ending in ***y***, change the ***y*** to ***i*** before adding the suffix.

2 a Write four comparing phrases that can be made from these. The first is done for you.

dangerous more dangerous most dangerous
less dangerous least dangerous

suspicious
reliable
generous
cautious

b Take one of the sets of comparing phrases that you have made and write sentences to show how the phrases can be used.

Tip

Use **more** or **less** to compare one thing with *one* other thing.

Use **most** or **least** to compare something with *more than one* other thing.

Making questions

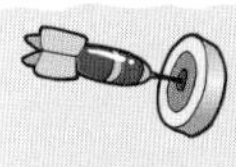

Sentence work

- To change sentences from statements to questions and questions to statements

Sentences can sometimes be changed from statements to questions, or vice versa, without changing many words.

Tip

Vice versa means *the other way round.*

Remember

Questions always need a **question mark**.

1 Write these statement sentences as questions. Change as few words as possible.

a The children in Victorian factories worked long hours.

b The workers were often ill-treated.

c Sickness was common among the child workers.

d Accidents often occurred.

e Some accidents were fatal.

2 Write these questions as statements. Change as few words as possible.

a Can you see the child under the machinery?

b Did they work weekends as well?

c Were the children tired from working long hours?

d Did tiredness cause some of the accidents?

e Were the new factory laws helpful in making the owners act more responsibly?

Helpful words

What Where
When Will
Why How
Did Would

Word work

- To practise end of word letter patterns

ary, ery, ory word endings

I read in a library about the dangerous machinery in a Victorian factory.

These three letter patterns sound very similar, and cause spelling problems!

1 Use a dictionary to help you finish each of these words with an *ary*, *ery* or *ory* letter pattern:

a *necess*_____ **b** *fact*_____
c *brav*_____ **d** *discov*_____
e *ordin*_____ **f** *diction*_____
g *mem*_____ **h** *nurs*_____
i *brib*_____ **j** *burgl*_____
k *gl*_____ **l** *extraordin*_____

Remember

To make the plural of most nouns ending in ***y***, change the ***y*** to ***i*** and add ***es***.

2 Write the plural forms of each of these words:

a *secretary* **b** *delivery*
c *story* **d** *dictionary*
e *burglary* **f** *victory*
g *discovery* **h** *brewery*
i *mystery* **j** *boundary*
k *memory* **l** *salary*

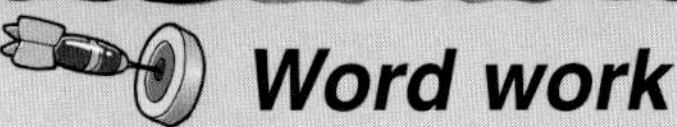

Word work

- To revise antonyms and synonyms

Word pairs

Remember, thinking about antonyms and synonyms can help to improve our writing, e.g.

dangerous *perilous* (synonym) *safe* (antonym)

1 Find in the wordsearch a synonym for each of these words.
ugly large work sleep

Add another yourself.

Remember

A **synonym** has a similar meaning; an **antonym** has the opposite meaning.

z	p	o	k	c	r	s	e	b
s	l	u	m	b	e	r	t	e
m	e	v	a	r	l	d	n	a
a	r	v	s	l	a	a	o	u
l	h	n	s	v	x	m	p	t
l	t	o	i	l	i	k	l	i
u	t	c	v	w	p	o	w	f
w	a	k	e	m	l	c	v	u
h	i	d	e	o	u	s	n	l

2 Find in the wordsearch an antonym for each of the words.

er, ier, est and *iest* word endings

Handwriting

er ier est iest er ier est iest er ier est iest er ier est iest

1 **a** Practise the letter patterns three times.

b Write a word that has each of the suffix endings that you have been practising.

2 Neatly copy these sentences, adding a word from the brackets to fill each gap:

a *He works _____ than me. He is the _____ worker in our factory. (harder hardest)*

b *I am the _____ runner in our street. I can even run _____ than my dad. (faster fastest)*

c *He is very silly. He is the _____ person I know, _____ even than my little brother! (sillier silliest)*

Unit 19

Book Covers

Sentence work

- To choose the best words for each context

Choosing adjectives

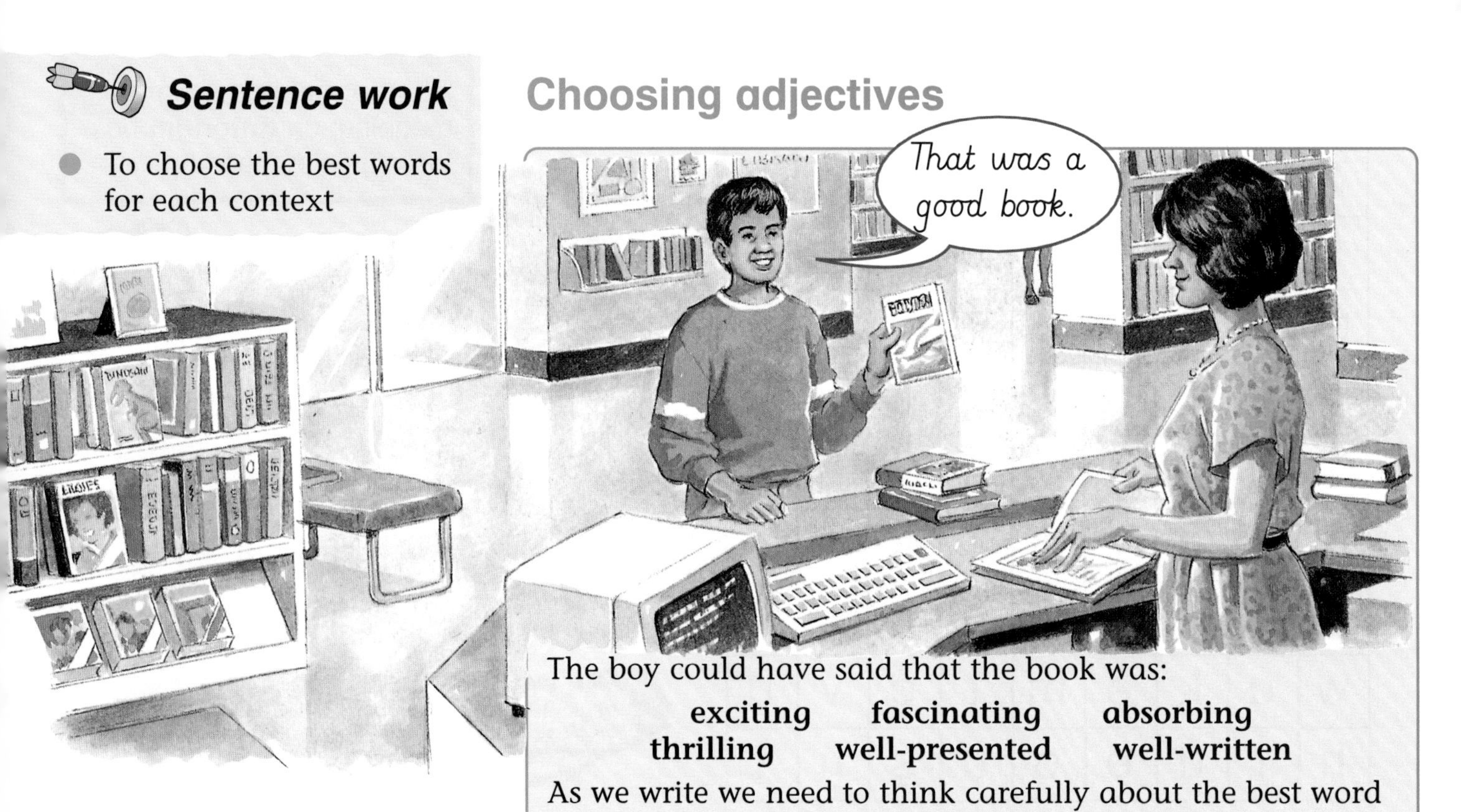

The boy could have said that the book was:

exciting **fascinating** **absorbing**
thrilling **well-presented** **well-written**

As we write we need to think carefully about the best word that describes what we want to tell our readers.

1 Choose the best word from the brackets to complete these sentences:

a "How much is this book, please? I would like to (buy / get / obtain / purchase / procure / acquire) a copy," said the boy.

b "It's quite (cheap / inexpensive / mean / low-cost)," said the assistant.

c "I'll have (a couple / two / a pair / a duo of) copies then please. One for me and one for my (pal / mate / chum / friend / companion / comrade / confidant / partner)," (said / explained / replied / responded / retorted) the boy.

d "I am (sure / certain / positive / satisfied / convinced / confident) you'll both be (pleased / happy / content / satisfied / gratified) with it," he said.

2 **a** Make a list of adverbs that could be used to describe:

how children walk to school

how children sit in chairs

how they go upstairs

how they run around the playground

b Write sentences using some of the words you have collected to describe how *you* like to do each of these things.

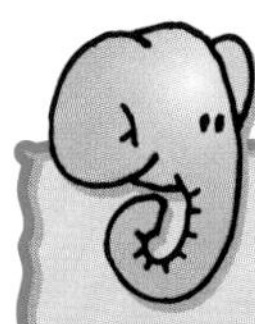

Remember

Adverbs tell us more about verbs.

Using commas in lists

Sentence work

- To revise the use of commas in writing lists

I borrowed some books for my homework about castles, knights, weapons, the Tudors and walled towns.

Remember, when writing lists we put a comma between each item, except before the last where we put **and** or **or**.

1 Add the missing commas in these lists:

a *Joe collects books about football cricket swimming cycling skate-boarding and fishing.*

b *On our shelf we have books about the countries we have visited, including Scotland Wales England France Spain Italy and Jersey.*

c *I'm not sure whether my favourite author is Roald Dahl Jane Gardam Laxman Komal Pat Moon or J. K. Rowling.*

2 As well as adding the missing commas in these sentences, check and correct the rest of the punctuation and use of capital letters:

a *Our teacher has asked us to find information about cities the romans lived in, such as london winchester chester york lincoln and bath*

b *Ive asked several people to help me, including joe salma mark jessica anila and ben*

Word work

- To extend ideas for mnemonics

Tip

The best mnemonics are the ones you make up for yourself.

Mnemonics

Mnemonics can help us to remember how to spell tricky words.

1 Copy these words and underline the part each mnemonic helps us to remember:

a *thieves* — *thieves tell lies*
b *truly* — *July is truly summer*
c *vegetable* — *we get vegetables for our table*
d *weight* — *the weight of eight plates*
e *separate* — *means to part*
f *siege* — *people can die in a siege*
g *witch* — *which witch can make you itch?*

2 Make up your own mnemonics for these tricky words, or choose six others that you especially want to remember:

a jealous **b** suspicious
c thoughtful **d** contented
e accommodation **f** delicious

Using a dictionary

1 Use a dictionary to help to solve this puzzle:

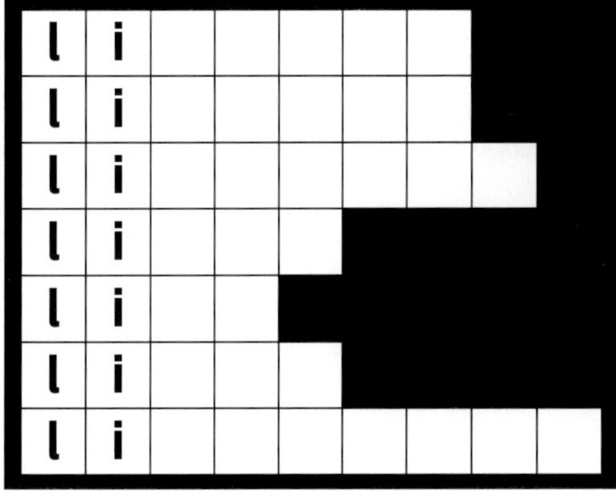

l	i								a room for books
l	i								a permit
l	i								a rescue vessel
l	i								brightness so one can see
l	i								to be fond of
l	i								a large passenger ship
l	i								a black sweet

2 Make up a similar puzzle yourself, for a friend to solve.

Word work

- To practise dictionary skills

Lettering a book cover

The layout and lettering on a book cover are very important. Readers are only tempted to look inside a book and read it if they are first attracted by the cover.

Book designers need to think about:

- whether to use capital letters or lower case letters
- whether to arrange the title and picture in the centre, or to one side
- whether to have a picture or a pattern on the cover

1 Look at the cover of a book that you have been reading recently. Make a list of the things that you think are good, and another list of what you think are less good.

2 Draw the shape of a book, and on it plan the cover for a book called THE MYSTERY OF THE DINOSAURS. Pretend that you are the author.

Arrange the lettering very neatly, using faint guide lines to keep it neat and even.

Handwriting

Tip

Lower case letters are the letters that are not capital letters, sometimes called *small* letters.

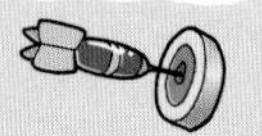

Unit 20

Fitness Exercises

Sentence work

- To revise the main verb tenses

Tenses

Remember, there are three main tenses that tell us when the action of a sentence takes place – in the **future**, at the **present** time or in the **past**.

1 Read these present tense sentences. Write them again, but in the past tense. The first one is done for you.

a *I like football.*
I liked football.

b *I have a new, clean white football.*

c *This is my new football shirt.*

d *It is clean and fresh for the match.*

e *I am feeling excited.*

2 Read these past tense sentences. Write them again, but in the future tense. The first one is done for you.

a *It was a good match.*
It is going to be a good match.

b *United was a strong team.*

c *Our team was more than able to take them on.*

d *Our goalkeeper was very good, so there was no chance they would score.*

e *We won easily, and are the new champions.*

Commas in sentences

Sentence work

- To practise using commas to mark boundaries in sentences

While standing, slowly rotate your head clockwise and anticlockwise.

Commas are important in instructions. The comma tells the reader when to pause slightly for the sentence to make most sense.

1 Without looking at the passage in the Comprehension and Writing Skills book, copy these sentences putting in the commas that have been omitted:

a *Stand straight and raise both your shoulders together then push down.*

b *Now lift one shoulder up and down then the other.*

c *Now swing your arms back and forth then rotate them in large circles.*

d *With your arms by your sides stand upright with your feet together.*

e *Jump with your arms and legs outstretched then bring them back again.*

2 Neatly copy these paragraphs putting in the commas that have been omitted:

Touching your toes

From a standing position slowly reach down and touch your toes keeping your legs straight. Now stand up again.

Ankle clasps

Keeping your legs straight bend down and clasp one ankle with both hands. Slowly push your head down. towards your hands holding for ten seconds then repeat using the other ankle.

Word work

- To practise the *ie, ei* spelling rule

Tip

Try to learn this rule off by heart – it is worth remembering.

ie and *ei* spellings

This rule will help you to remember whether ***i*** comes before or after ***e***:

- ***i*** comes before ***e*** — pi**e**ce, rel**ie**f
- except after ***c*** — rec**ei**ve, c**ei**ling
- or when the sound is not ***ee*** — forf**ei**t, **ei**ght

receipt eight vein shield chief
deceit field sleight their receive
wield achieve rein believe leisure

1 Copy all the words in the box in which the ***ie*** or ***ei*** sounds like *ee* in *bee*. What do you notice about the ***ei*** words in your list?

2 Copy the words in which the ***ie*** or ***ei*** does not sound like *ee* in *bee*. What do you notice about these words?

Word work

- To find and use homophones

Homophones

Remember, **homophones** sound the same but have different spellings and meanings.

1 In this wordsearch are five sets of homophones. Copy them out in pairs.

v	e	i	n	w	a	y
z	i	r	w	p	c	s
r	g	e	e	v	n	l
a	h	i	i	a	t	e
i	t	g	g	i	e	i
n	o	n	h	n	t	g
s	l	a	y	s	u	h

2 Choose three pairs, and write three sentences which, like the one in the teaching box, include both homophones.

ief and *eight* patterns

ief eight ief eight ief eight ief eight ief eight ief eight

1 **a** Practise the letter patterns three times.

b Neatly copy these words twice each:

chief relief belief thief grief

eight weight freight height

2 **a** Neatly copy the silly sentence:

We gave the thief grief when we dropped a weight on his head from a great height.

b Make your own funny sentence using ***ie*** and ***ei*** words.

Weather

Sentence work

- To practise extending sentences

Expanding sentences

January new beginning,
Resolutions,
Snowflakes spinning.

Poets are good at using a few words to capture a picture of a scene or the mood of a situation.

But when we are writing, we often need longer, more descriptive sentences.

January is the first month of the new year, the fresh-start month, when many people make new year resolutions, promising 'not to ...' and 'this year I really will ...'.

It is also the month for the white, silent snowfall of winter, the stunning beauty of snow-clad trees, whitened buildings and carpeted roads and gardens.

January is the month of snowmen, snowballs, toboggans – and the month when the weather may be so bad that we can't get to school!

1 Write an expanded version of this verse of the poem:

April showers fall soft and slow,
Earth wakes up,
And green things grow.

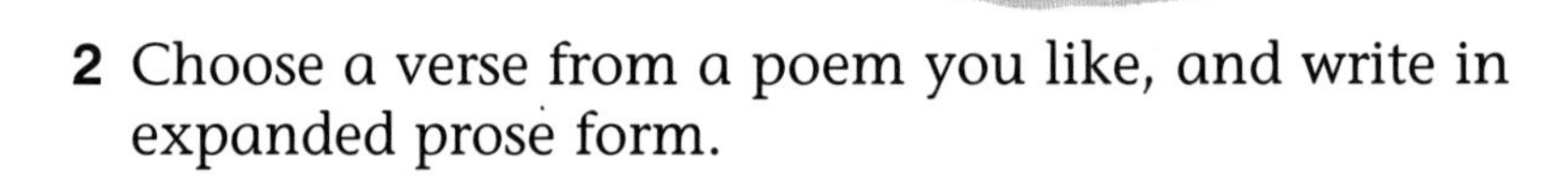

2 Choose a verse from a poem you like, and write in expanded prose form.

Tip

Prose is when we are not writing poetry!

Headlines

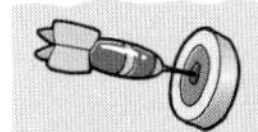

Sentence Work

- To practise summarising to make headlines

WORST SNOW IN JAN FOR 50 YEARS

Headlines are at the beginning of newspaper and magazine articles. They summarise the main point of the article in very few words.

Tip

Headlines are often dramatic – to get you to buy the newspaper and read the news.

1 Write a dramatic headline that could have been written during each of the other months of the year.

2 Look at a page of a newspaper.

a Copy the headline that catches your attention most.

b Write a few sentences to explain whether you think it is a good headline, and accurately summarises the main point of the article.

c Write headlines of your own for some of the other stories in the newspaper.

Tip

Headlines are sometimes in capital letters.

Word work

- To revise the spelling of important words with silent letters

Silent letters

> *May Day ribbons round a pole,*
> *May-time babies*
> *Lamb and foal.*
>
> Some letters don't make a sound when read, like **b** in *lamb*.

1 These words look wrong. All the silent letters have been left out. Copy out the words, adding the missing letters where they are needed. The first one has been done for you.

a rubarb rhubarb **b** plumer
c gost **d** tonge
e thum **f** onestly
g lisen **h** casle
i thisle **j** anser
k reckage **l** rench
m desiner **n** ryme
o nat **p** crum

Tip

Some of these words *start* with a silent letter.

2 Neatly copy this passage, putting back the silent letters omitted where there is a *:

Despite her r*eumatism, Gran *nelt down to smel* the s*ent of the flowers. She had an extensiv* *nowledge of plants, and w*en she was y*unger had *rit*en a g*ide book. Now she was old and *rinkled, she would stil* spend *ours ans*ering our q*estions. Nothing could disg*ise how much she *new.

Word work

- To make clues for a crossword puzzle

Crossword puzzles

Crossword puzzles are fun brain-teasers.
This one has already been completed.
It is mainly about the seasons and the countryside.

1 Make up clues for the puzzle in the box.
Three have been done for you.

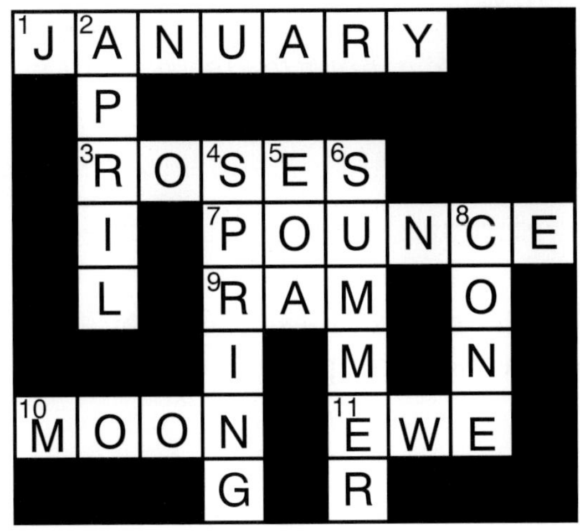

Clues for words going across

1 The first month in the year.
3
7
9
10
11

Clues for words going down

2 The month famous for its showers.
4
5 The second, fourth and first vowel letters.
6
8

2 Make up your own crossword puzzle using words about a subject in which you are interested.

Using capitals

Handwriting

A B C D E F G H I J K L M N O P Q R S T U V W X Y Z

1 Write a headline, neatly in capital letters, for the most exciting thing that has happened to you recently.

2 Write the headline, in capitals, for something you would most like to happen in the near future, such as your team winning the championship!

Netiquette

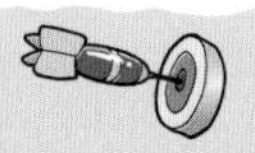

Sentence work

- To revise the importance of ordering clauses in the best way

Tip

Adding a clause *within a sentence* is called **embedding the clause**.

Improving sentences

My friend, <u>who is a computer expert</u>, has been teaching me how to use e-mail.

This could have been written:

My friend has been teaching me how to use e-mail. He is a computer expert.

But the first version flows better.

We say that the clause underlined has been **embedded**.

1 Rewrite these pairs of sentences as one sentence by embedding a clause, as in the example in the box:

a *My friend knows more about computers than me. She is younger than me.*

b *The software wouldn't work. It was rather complicated.*

c *If Ali couldn't fix it, I knew I couldn't. He knows much more than I do about computers.*

d *Eventually he made it connect. It took hours of patient work.*

e *I enjoy sending e-mail messages to my friends. I send both long chatty messages and short brief ones.*

2 These short, simple sentences could be made much more interesting. Write them again, adding another embedded clause where the * appears, to give the reader more information.

a *My uncle * walked in the door carrying a big box.*

b *I couldn't wait to open the box * but Mum said I must finish my food first!*

c *It was a new computer * and a complete surprise.*

d *I've always wanted a faster computer * and now I have one!*

e *Joe * will be very jealous.*

Punctuation practice

Sentence work

- To revise the key punctuation marks and use of capital letters

1 Add the missing capital letters and punctuation marks to this passage. To make life difficult (as it is the last unit in the book) the word spaces have also been left out. Good luck!

whenmumanddadsawwhatunclematthadboughtme formybirthdaytheyweresurprisedunclemattisalways generousbuttogivemeanewcomputerwasamazingjoe mybestfriendcouldntbelieveitmyothergoodfriendali askedifhecouldbuymyoldone

2 Copy this extract, adding the missing speech marks and commas, and beginning a new line whenever necessary:

You are extremely lucky said Joe because that model has only just come out. I know I replied and it isn't my birthday for another three weeks. Why did your uncle matt give it to you now then? I'm not sure I said but I think it is because he has to go away for a few weeks and wanted to see my face when I opened the box. I wish I had an uncle like that laughed joe.

Remember

Begin a new line whenever a different person starts to speak.

Word work

- To revise the main patterns containing *gh*

gh letter patterns

> OK everybody, sit up str**aight**! It's about time we t**aught** you some manners.

The ***gh*** patterns are worth practising, as they often occur in English words, and can be tricky!

Helpful words

night fright
fight thigh
might bright
light right

1 Write an ***igh*** word to answer each of these clues:

a Perhaps I will, I ________

b When owls hoot

c Antonym of both heavy and dark

d Sudden fear

e Antonym of dim

f Upper part of the leg

g Antonym for left

h A violent squabble

Helpful words

through thought
trough rough
cough fought
bough borough
fought throughout
brought bought
dough thorough
enough though
plough ought
drought

2 a Make a list of as many words as you can with ***ough*** in them, and sort them into groups in which the ***gh*** letter pattern sounds like:

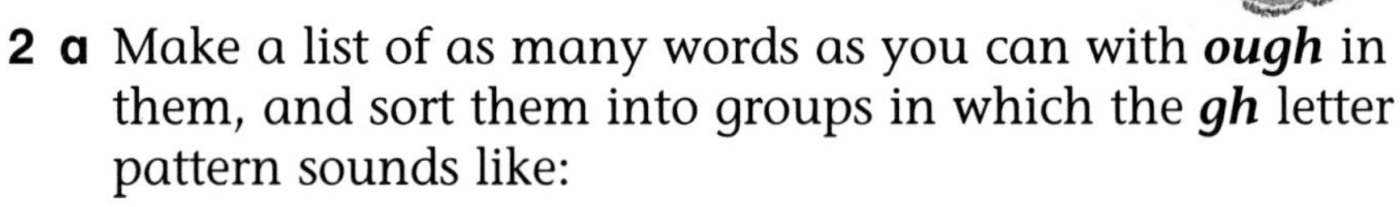

b List any words with the ***ough*** pattern that don't fit into your lists.

c Write a nonsense sentence that uses as many of these ***augh*** words as you can fit into it!

daughter caught taught slaughter naughty
laugh laughing laughter draught

Invented words

Keypals Just like penpals – only you write to them using a keyboard, not a pen.

Newbie Someone who is new to the Net.

Flame A crushing put-down or nasty remark.

Flamebait Someone who deserves to be flamed!

When something new is invented we need new words to talk about it. Most new, or invented, words are built from words we already use.

Word work

- To demonstrate how words are sometimes created

Tip

Some words are the same, but are given different meanings, like *flame*.

1 Some new words have been created by joining two existing words, or parts of two existing words, together. Which words were used to make these words? The first two are done for you.

e-mail – electronic mail

newscast – news broadcast

heliport keypal chickenburger smog

2 a The suffix ***holic*** has come to mean being addicted to something. An alco**holic** is a person who drinks lots of alcohol.

Make up names for people who are addicted to: playing football; reading; talking; television; computer games.

b The suffix ***phobia*** means *fear of.*
Make up six words that have the suffix ***phobia***.

Designing an invitation

1 Plan and design an invitation for a party.
You are having a class celebration, and you want as many people as possible to come.

Decide:

- what you want to say on the invitation
- which words are most important
- which words will be in capital letters, and which in lower case

2 If possible, now design a similar invitation using a computer. Write some sentences explaining the advantages and disadvantages of using the computer for the invitations.

Handwriting

PEARSON EDUCATION LIMITED
Edinburgh Gate, Harlow, Essex, CM20 2JE, England
and Associated companies throughout the World.

First published 2000
Third impression 2002

Printed in China GCC/03
ISBN 0 582 40839 3

Acknowledgements
We are grateful to Mary Evans for permission to reproduce the photographs on pages 9 and 76.

The handwriting characters in this book were created using *Handwriting for Windows 2.0*. This product enables the user to create model handwriting in the size, colour and style of their choice (including a dotted script). HfW2 runs on Windows 95 and above and is available from KBER (Kath Balcombe Educational Resources). Please contact Customer Services for details on 01743 356764.

Cover Oxford Scientific Films (Frank Krahmer)

The publisher's policy is to use paper manufactured from sustainable forests.